Harvard Publications in Music

Harvard Publications in Music, 8

THE OPERAS OF ALESSANDRO SCARLATTI

Donald Jay Grout, General Editor

Volume III

THE OPERAS OF ALESSANDRO SCARLATTI

Volume III

GRISELDA

Edited by Donald Jay Grout
Elizabeth B. Hughes, Associate Editor

Harvard University Press
Cambridge, Massachusetts
and
London, England
1975

Publication of this book has been aided by a grant from
the Hull Memorial Publication Fund of Cornell University

Library of Congress Cataloging in Publication Data
Scarlatti, Alessandro, 1660–1725.
    Griselda.
    (The Operas of Alessandro Scarlatti ; v. 3)
(Harvard publications in music ; v. 8)
    Libretto by Apostolo Zeno.
    1. Operas—Scores.   I. Grout, Donald Jay.
II. Hughes, Elizabeth B   III. Zeno, Apostolo,
1668–1750.   Griselda.   IV. Title.   V. Harvard
publications in music ; v. 8.
M1500.S28G5 1975   782.1′54   75–5737
ISBN 0–674–64029–2

Acknowledgments

Acknowledgment is made with thanks to the following libraries for permission to use or reproduce manuscript material in their possession: The Trustees of the British Museum, London; Bibliothek des Bischöflichen Priesterseminars, Münster; Staatsbibliothek Preussischer Kulturbesitz, Berlin (West); Bibliothèque Nationale, Paris; Library of Congress, Washington; Bibliothèque du Conservatoire Royal de Musique, Brussels.

I wish to express thanks to the National Endowment for the Humanities and to Cornell University for grants in aid of research and for acquisition of material, to the Hull Memorial Publication Fund of Cornell University for a grant in aid of publication costs, and to colleagues and students at Cornell University, especially to Professor Robert A. Hall, Jr., for translation of the libretto and to Dr. and Mrs. Edward Swenson for assistance in preparation of the edition. I also wish to thank the following persons who have kindly responded to requests for information: Professor Claudio Sartori, Biblioteca Nazionale Braidense, Milan; Professor Edwin Hanley, University of California at Los Angeles; and Dr. Friedrich Lippman, Istituto Storico Germanico, Rome.

"Cloudbank"
Spafford, New York

D.J.G.

Contents

Contents

Contents

INTRODUCTION

Griselda in Early Opera

The type of Patient Griselda had flourished in folklore long before the lady herself made her formal debut in western literature, in the concluding tale of Boccaccio's *Decameron*. Since then, this paragon of patience and model of wifely submission has touched the imagination of Petrarch, Chaucer, Hans Sachs, Thomas Dekker, Lope de Vega, Ferrault, Goldoni, Gerhart Hauptmann, and dozens of other authors up to modern times. As Boccaccio tells it, the story represents Griselda simply as a poor peasant girl married to a great lord who, having capriciously chosen her as a wife, proceeds to submit her to a series of trials in order to prove her obedience. Enduring all with unfailing patience and unwavering devotion to her tyrannical husband, she finally softens his heart and is graciously restored to his affections.

For the theater the bare tale of Griselda's tribulations obviously had to be supplemented. Dramatists from Dekker onward have tried to assign some rational motive for the husband's conduct; they have sought to make Griselda herself more credible by emphasizing the inner struggles she undergoes in her efforts to satisfy her lord's outrageous demands; and they have embroidered the action with all sorts of secondary personages and episodes in order to provide occasion for varied dramatic confrontations. In some seventeenth century dramas these additions were carried to ridiculous extremes. More moderate was the version constructed by Apostolo Zeno for the libretto of the first Griselda opera, staged at Venice in 1701 with music by Antonio Pollarolo.

Zeno (1668–1750)—man of letters, savant, poet at the Imperial court of Vienna from 1718 to 1729, author (alone or in collaboration) of texts for thirty-six operas and seventeen oratorios—was a favorite librettist in the first two decades of the eighteenth century. *Griselda* was one of his most successful works; with various modifications, it was set to music by some fifteen different composers in the first twenty years of its existence and furnished the substantial basis for at least twenty more operas in the course of the eighteenth century. As worked out by Zeno, with details borrowed from Boccaccio and other authors, the plot is as follows:

Griselda, daughter of a humble peasant, is the wife of Gualtiero, King of Sicily. Two children have been born to them: a daughter, who was kidnapped from the cradle fifteen years before the action of the drama begins and whom Griselda believes dead, and a son, now in infancy. The birth of the latter has brought to a head a movement of revolt among Gualtiero's nobles, who have always objected to Griselda because of her lowly origin and who are now openly rebellious at the prospect of being one day ruled by the grandson of a peasant. Gualtiero resolves to prove to them that Griselda's virtuous character makes her worthy to be their queen and mother of their future king. For that purpose he subjects his beloved wife to a series of public ordeals and humiliations, himself secretly sorrowing all the while but confident that the spectacle of Griselda's patient endurance will finally win over the reluctant vassals. The play opens with Gualtiero's formal repudiation of Griselda, amid the approving shouts of his followers. He tells Griselda that he has caused their daughter to be killed and that now he intends to take another wife, this time one of noble birth who will be worthy of her royal rank. At this moment arrive a young couple, Roberto and Costanza, under the escort of Corrado, Roberto's older brother and the confidential servant of Gualtiero. Roberto and Costanza are in love; but now they despair, because they believe it is Costanza who has been chosen to be Gualtiero's bride. This, however—as we are allowed to guess from veiled allusions in the dialogue—is not the true state of affairs: Costanza is really the long-lost daughter whom Gualtiero had sent away in infancy to be reared by relatives in a far city; she has now grown out of recognition, and her real identity is known only to Gualtiero and Corrado.

Meanwhile, Griselda's troubles are multiplying. Ottone, one of Gualtiero's courtiers, pursues her with entreaties and promises, hoping to gain her for his wife now that she is no longer queen. Under pretended orders from Gualtiero, Ottone threatens to kill Griselda's little son Everardo; he will spare the child, he says, if Griselda will marry him, but Griselda will not yield. (Ottone never carries out his threat.) Costanza chances upon Griselda in her lowly cottage, the childhood home to which she has returned after being banished from court. The two feel a mutual interest and sympathy, without knowing the cause. At Costanza's request, Gualtiero consents to receive Griselda in the palace, but only in the capacity of serving woman to his new wife. After Griselda, amid insults and abuse, has dutifully prepared everything for the wedding of Gualtiero and Costanza, Gualtiero imposes the supreme test of obedience: Griselda must marry Ottone. For the first time, Griselda refuses to submit; she prefers death at the hands of her true lord to such dishonor. Satisfied at last, Gualtiero embraces her and reveals to the assembled nobles the real motive of his conduct; all shout "Viva Griselda." Costanza's identity is disclosed, and Ottone confesses that it was he who fomented the revolt in hope of winning Griselda. Gualtiero forgives him, Roberto and Costanza are united, and all ends happily.

One can hardly rank Zeno among the great dramatists, though *Griselda* is a model of economy, realism, and lucidity compared to many opera plots of the seventeenth and eighteenth centuries. But Zeno's characters are singularly unconvincing. Griselda herself, to be sure, is hardly meant to be a "real" person; she appears as simply the embodiment *à outrance* of wifely submission and patience. Gualtiero, however, is no more credible; Zeno's best efforts cannot make him sympathetic to a modern age that has ceased to admire the ideal of the magnanimous tyrant and autocratic husband. Ottone is a stage villain. Only Roberto and Costanza bear any resemblance to real human beings. The anonymous arranger of Scarlatti's libretto made this traditional pair of young lovers considerably more conspicuous and drew them with a finer hand than Zeno had done; he eliminated one of Zeno's personages, a superfluous comic servant; furthermore, he improved many details of Zeno's text, making out of it a far more effective opera libretto while retaining the basic structure and much of the wording of the original.[1]

1. See D. J. Grout, "La 'Griselda' di Zeno e il libretto dell'opera di Scarlatti" in *Nuova Rivista Musicale Italiana*, II (1968): 23–40.

The Structure of Scarlatti's *Griselda*

The artificiality of *Griselda* must be understood as conforming to the demands of an age that sought in the musical theater not only spectacle to delight the eye and music to delight the ear (though these were naturally of prime importance) but also entertainment organized in conventional, familiar, stylized form—entertainment, moreover, with moral significance, presenting certain traits of character and conduct which could be accepted, if not necessarily as examples for imitation or avoidance, at least as models to be contemplated with edification or disapproval. Whether the action and personages were plausible was a minor consideration. The main requirements for an opera libretto were that it should offer convenient occasions for the display of varied feelings, moods, or "affections," and that the occasions for such displays in song be properly distributed throughout the opera and properly divided among the different singers.

The structure of Scarlatti's opera is admirably designed to satisfy the requirements of both form and expression. After an orchestral overture, its three acts consist of an almost unvarying succession of recitatives and solo arias. The recitatives embody the action in dialogue (rarely, in soliloquy); periodically, when the action reaches an appropriate point, one of the actors in the scene delivers himself of an aria expressing the sentiments or reflections to which the current situation supposedly gives rise in his mind; after his aria, as a rule, he leaves the stage and a new scene begins. The recitative is accompanied by a harpsichord and one or more instruments sustaining the bass line; it has a minimum of melodic or other musical organization, being for the most part a highly stylized version of ordinary speech, performed with all the speed and rhythmic flexibility of spoken words. Occasional expressive touches may be found in the midst of the harmonic and melodic clichés with which the recitatives abound, and at moments of special dramatic tension, as in the final scene of Act III, the recitative may be accompanied by sustained chords in the string orchestra. But the principal musical interest of the opera lies in the arias. Accompanied always by the orchestra, subtly organized musically, their most obvious formal feature is a division into two parts, the second shorter than the first though usually closely related to it in both text and music. After this second part, the first is repeated *da capo*—not literally but with additional melodic embellishments inserted at will by the singer.

Scarlatti's *Griselda* has no role for a bass. The only tenor is Corrado, a minor personage. Griselda, Roberto, and Costanza are sopranos, Gualtiero and Ottone contraltos. Male soprano and contralto roles were usually sung by castrati, female roles by women; but because at Rome in Scarlatti's time women were not allowed to appear on the stage, the entire cast of *Griselda* (except for Corrado) was made up of castrati. These singers were one of the peculiar institutions of seventeenth and eighteenth century Italian musical life; the best of them—such as Carestini, who made his public debut as Costanza in *Griselda*—possessed a fabulous technique and were adept at decorating a composer's written melodic line with vocal embellishments and adding cadenzas at certain places in an aria. Such decorations were expected; they were, at least in principle, improvised and thus could be different at each performance. As a consequence of this practice the actual sound of the arias, particularly of those in slow tempo, was considerably more elaborate than the notes of the score might suggest.

As far as its outward structure is concerned, *Griselda* conforms quite closely to the type of *opera seria* that was being cultivated by younger Italian composers in the 1720s. That it never became widely popular was doubtless due to its musical style, which is that of the late baroque—a style that had gone out of fashion in Italy by 1720, though Handel was able to maintain it in his own way for another ten or fifteen years at London. Scarlatti's popularity as an opera composer had been at its height in the 1690s and around the turn of the century; after 1702 his rate of production of dramatic works declined, though he remained active and was highly regarded as a composer of church music and cantatas. After a last series of operas written at Rome between 1718 and 1722 he virtually went into retirement at Naples, where he died in October of 1725. But the very qualities that mitigated against the success of the operas produced in the last years of his life are among those that have caused them to be admired by later generations. Scarlatti's case is somewhat parallel to that of J. S. Bach who, though respected as a "learned" composer, was regarded as hopelessly old-fashioned by his progressive younger contemporaries.

Sources

Of Scarlatti's reputed 115 operas, *Griselda* (1721) is the last of which the music has been preserved. It comes to us in three principal manuscripts:

A   Autograph, Acts I and III only. London, British Museum Add. 14.168. 129 folios, 21 x 28 cm.

S   An eighteenth century Italian copy at Münster, Bibliothek des Bischöflichen Priesterseminars, Santini Hs. 3894. 27.5 x 20.5 cm.

B   An eighteenth century copy, also presumably Italian, at Berlin, Staatsbibliothek Preussischer Kulturbesitz, Musikabteilung, Mus. ms. 19640: 160 folios numbered in pencil, 21 x 27.5 cm. The title page has a stamp "Ex Biblioth. Regia Berolinensi" and the notation "der Königl. Bibl. geschenkt von S.W. Dehn Berlin, in Febr. 1843." The gatherings of 4 folios each are numbered in ink in the upper left-hand corner (Act I, 1–25; Act II, 1–23; Act III, 1–13).

Additional sources are:

P   An eighteenth century collection of nineteen arias and one duet, in full score, at Paris, Bibliothèque Nationale, D 11.898 and 5.487. 138 folios.

W   Washington, Library of Congress, M 1500. S 28 G 5. This manuscript, which was obtained in 1919 from W. Barclay Squire of London, consists of 180 numbered folios, 17 x 23 cm. On the first page (unnumbered) is a notation in an eighteenth century hand: "Quarta Opera che suonai il Cimbalo in Capranica." Folios 1–135v contain, in random order, twenty arias, two duets, and one quartet from *Griselda*, together with a portion of the accompanied recitative from the final scene, all in full score. With the exception of this recitative, one duet (Number 60), and two arias (Number 29 and 47), the contents of *W* are the same as those of *P* (though in different order), and the latter contains no items that are not also in *W*. From folio 57 on, the hand is that of the same scribe who wrote all of *P*. The large number of common errors and variants (see Critical Notes,[2] especially to Number 37) suggests that these two manuscripts were copied either one from the other or both from the same source.

2. Available from the Department of Music, Harvard University.

W also contains, beginning at folio 136, nine arias and two duets from various operas by D. Sarro, Porpora, Gasperini, Auletti, Vignari, and G. Bononcini, with indications of dates (1719 to 1721) and places (Rome, Venice, Milan, Turin). Most interesting is an aria on folios 144–153v "Sciolta dal lido" by "Sr. Giuseppe Vignari di Milano." The vocal line is written on two separate staffs, the second of which professes to be the version sung by the famous soprano Faustina Bordoni at Milan in 1720 with her "modi" or ornaments. If this is an authentic transcript it provides a rare example of the way in which a singer at this time might have actually interpreted a composer's written line.[3]

The remaining known manuscripts of *Griselda* are copies of *B*:

Brussels, Bibliothèque du Conservatoire Royal de Musique, 2352.K
Washington, Library of Congress, M1500.S28 Gr6

Another manuscript, also probably a copy of *B*, formerly preserved in Bayrischer Staatsbibliothek at Munich, is reported as missing since the end of World War II.

Two arias, evidently copied from *P*, are in the Bibliothèque du Conservatoire at Brussels (Bc 4864, 4865), part of a set of twelve arias in an eighteenth century hand from various operas of Scarlatti. Three in this set are from *Il Trionfo dell'Onore* and five from *Laodicea e Berenice*; the remaining arias are not identified.

Only one printing of Scarlatti's libretto is known:

L *Griselda Dramma per Musica da recitarsi nella Sala dell'Ill.mo Sig. Federico Capranica nel Carnevale dell' Anno 1721 . . . In Roma, pe'Tinassi, MDCCXXI*, 89 pp.

The manuscripts used in preparing this edition are *A, S, B, W, P* (in photocopy), and *Bc* 4864–4865, along with an examplar of the libretto at Brussels, Conservatoire, Litt. UU 20.619.

As usual with operas of this period, there are many discrepancies between the libretto and the scores as well as among the scores themselves. Such variants are listed in detail in the Critical Notes, but the main classes of them may be summarized here:

(1) Many lines of recitative in *L* (42 in Act I, 65 in Act II, 11 in Act III) are "virgolated," that is marked with a double comma (,,) at the beginning to indicate omission. All such lines in Acts I and III have been set to music in *A* and later cancelled, either by crossing out or pasting over or both. Also composed and cancelled are about a dozen lines of recitative which do not appear anywhere in *L*.

(2) Three arias in *L* are marked with the sign ₓ*ₓ to indicate omission; two of these, as well as one other aria not so marked, have been set to music in *A* and cancelled. Furthermore, *A* contains one aria (likewise cancelled), the text of which does not appear anywhere in *L*.

(3) *A* also contains numerous long and short passages in recitatives, a few short passages in arias, and one entire aria which were cancelled and replaced with different versions.

(4) In the ritornellos of thirteen arias of Acts I and III fragments from one to five measures in length have been cancelled in *A*. Most such places seem to

---

3. Attention is called to an article by George J. Buelow "A Lesson in Operatic Performance by Madame Faustina Bordoni," scheduled to appear in a volume of essays in honor of Martin Bernstein published by the New York University Press. I wish to thank Professor Buelow for an advance copy of his essay, which includes a transcription of Faustina's ornaments for the aria by Vignari.

have been simply "abandoned continuations," but a few of them (notably in Numbers 5, 11, 17, and 86) might have been made only for the purpose of saving time; at any rate, they could be restored without completely destroying the musical sense of the passages in which they occur. The same is true of six measures deleted from the body of the aria "Ho in seno due fiammelle" (Number 81). However, in the entire musical context it seems clear that all these deletions are justified and should not be restored. While details can be established only for Acts I and III, it may be assumed that similar and probably equally extensive alterations were made in Act II.

None of the items or passages cancelled in *A* appear in either *S* or *B*, and neither scribe gives any indication that cancellations or changes had been made in the score from which he was copying. Both copies conform closely to the revised version of the autograph—*B* somewhat more closely in details than *S*. In effect, both are simply clean copies of a considerably revised and shortened version of the opera. Whether an original version was ever performed or whether the changes were made before the first performance we do not know. By evidence of the printed libretto, it was the revised version that was staged at the Teatro Capranico in Rome in January of 1721.[4]

When the autograph was rebound at the British Museum in March of 1966 all the pasteover slips were lifted off. The music thus revealed, as well as that which had been merely crossed out but remained still decipherable, will be found collected in the Appendix of this volume, with indication of its original place in the score.

Editorial Principles

Detailed reference to variants and peculiarities will be found in the Critical Notes. Obvious trivial errors have been corrected without notice. The following principles apply to this edition as a whole.

Most details of spelling, capitalization, punctuation, accents, and elision of syllables in the text of both recitatives and arias have been made to conform to modern Italian usage. Stage directions have been taken sometimes from the score, sometimes from the libretto.

Numbering of measures begins with the first complete measure of each item (aria, recitative, or sinfonia). Because of a conjecture (perhaps unjustified) that the beaming of eighth notes in the string parts may have some relation to the desired articulation, I have followed *A* in this respect for Acts I and III and *B* for Act II, indicating in the Critical Notes some though not all variant beamings. No slurs have been added. Tempo indications are as in the original, with abbreviations written out in full. Time signatures are as in the original except for omission of the superfluous C before 3/8 and other triple signatures. The last movement of the Sinfonia Number 1 and the arias Numbers 31 and 49, which have signatures in duple time with prevailing triplet division of the beat, have been transcribed in 6/8 to conform to the composer's intentions.

The original key signatures, which frequently have one less sharp or flat than in modern usage, have been retained. Accidentals are indicated according to modern practice. Clefs in instrumental parts are as in the original. Clefs in the

---

4. See D. J. Grout, "The Original Version of Scarlatti's *Griselda*" in *Essays on Opera and English Music in Honour of Sir Jack Westrup*, ed. Frederick Sternfeld, Nigel Fortune, and Edward Olleson (Oxford, Blackwell, 1975).

vocal parts have been changed to the treble G clef for the parts of Griselda, Roberto, and Costanza (originally soprano C clef) and of Gualtiero and Ottone (originally alto C clef), and to the tenor G clef for Corrado (originally tenor C clef).

The only dynamic indications in the original are *for:* and *pia:* (abbreviated in this edition to *f* and *p*). These are rarely found except in the accompaniments of arias; although they appear as a rule only in the first violin part, they are clearly meant to apply to all the parts. It is often uncertain which is the first note to be affected by them; in such cases the signs have been placed according to the editor's judgment, usually without special mention. No editorial dynamic markings have been added.

Where instruments are named in the original the names are retained, with modern spelling. For the exact original designations (reading from the top down) and for cases of unusual arrangement of the score (for example, woodwinds below strings), see the Critical Notes. Designations not in the original, as well as all other editorial markings, are italicized.

Figuring of the basso continuo follows the original; the few editorially added figures are enclosed in parentheses. Figures applying to all of a group of repeated bass notes have been placed under the first note of each group. The composite figure $\frac{4}{3}$ (usual at V-I cadences in recitatives and frequent at I$\frac{6}{4}$ –V– I cadences in arias) has been retained in recitatives but elsewhere rendered as two separate figures. Figures indefinitely placed in the original have been placed where they belong according to the editor's judgment. Except for the foregoing, all deviations from the original figuring are listed in the Critical Notes.

In all the manuscripts it is customary to divide a 4/4 measure after the second beat at the end of a system whenever convenient. Thus it happens that the bass will be notated in one source as two tied half notes, or a quarter note tied to a half note, or a half to a quarter, while in another the same bass will be notated as a whole note or a dotted half note. In such cases in the arias the single longer note rather than the tied shorter notes has been tacitly accepted for this edition. When the matter cannot be decided by comparison of sources (as when all the manuscripts happen to divide the same measure at the end of a line), the decision has usually been likewise in favor of the one longer note; but doubtful cases have been mentioned in the Critical Notes. All ties not necessitated by a divided measure have of course been retained. In the recitatives, all bass note ties without exception have been retained; in the recitatives of Acts I and III, ties necessitated by a divided measure in the autograph are indicated by the special sign ᵦ . The sign ᵦ signifies an editorially added slur or tie.

Some Notes on Performance Practice

The present edition aims to present an accurate full score of *Griselda* as delivered by the composer. It does not aim to incorporate every additional detail that might be required in an edition intended to be used by present-day performers because, in the first place, with respect to many such details our knowledge is imperfect; in the second place, the essence of such additions to the written score is that they were improvised, which means that no two performances in the eighteenth century would have been identical. To fix such details in print is to "freeze" one particular interpretation of the score which, given the present imperfect state of our knowledge, may be historically incorrect and which in any case is contrary to the ideal and practice of improvisatory freedom that ruled in the original performances of these works. Of course conductors, singers, and players who undertake to revive a Scarlatti opera nowadays must commit themselves more or less rigidly to a single interpretation; but no such single, fixed interpretation can ever be regarded as "definitive." Still, although many details of performance are uncertain, some general guidelines applying to the present score may be laid down with reasonable assurance.

Instruments

As a rule, oboes double the violin parts in the *forte* sections of aria accompaniments. Specific indications of this practice are rare in the sources, but an example occurs in Number 49 where the two principal manuscript copies (doubtless in accordance with the autograph) show exactly where the oboes are to play. The basso continuo is always sustained by one or more violoncellos in addition to the cembalo; in accompaniments which include wind instruments, and in *forte* passages generally, a bassoon also sustains the bass line. The cembalo is silent only where "senza cembalo" is specifically indicated and (probably) in passages where the bass line is written in the tenor clef. Such passages are always marked "solo" and with one exception (see Critical Notes to the duet Number 86) are unfigured in the autograph of *Griselda*.

Rhythm

Certain peculiarities of eighteenth century notation are to be observed. In a movement where the prevailing division of the beat is triple, dotted figures as a rule have to be "assimilated" to this triple division. Transcriptions in the present edition of the last movement of the Sinfonia and of the arias Numbers 31 and 49 have been made accordingly. The same rule should be applied to Number 17, where most of the combinations ♩. ♪ or equivalent become ♩ ³ ♪, and to the ritornellos (but not elsewhere) in Number 91. Conversely, notated triplets, especially in instrumental parts, often must be made to conform to a prevailing duple beat division, as in the "Sinfonia per lo sbarco," Number 12, and the aria Number 51; triplets in the voice part of Number 53 should also probably be resolved in this way. Dotted eighth notes in vigorous, lively rhythms should usually be "over-dotted" (see Introduction to *Eraclea*, Vol. I of this series). The aria Number 69 in *Griselda* is a good example for the application of this rule.

Recitative

The C time signature in the notation of recitative is purely conventional and has nothing to do with rhythm or phrasing. The recitative was probably half sung, half spoken, in brisk tempo fluctuating in accord with the natural tempo of speech and with fine careless disregard of the exact notated pitches and rhythms except at cadences.

The frequent dominant–tonic cadences in recitative practically always occur in one or the other of two standard forms:

Since the middle of the eighteenth century it has been customary at such places to postpone sounding the dominant–tonic chords of the accompaniment until after the singer finishes the phrase. This, however, seems not to have been the rule in Italian opera recitative in Scarlatti's time; it is more likely that the resolution took place simultaneously in voice and accompaniment, as a literal reading of the notation would prescribe. (The two successive sharp dissonances between voice and accompaniment that result when the cadence occurs in form *a* are much less noticeable with a cembalo than with a modern pianoforte.) In addition, there is some evidence that the penultimate note of the bass could have carried above it in effect a single compound chord combining tonic and dominant elements, for example,

and that the compound figure $\frac{4}{3}$, which Scarlatti invariably writes at definitive dominant–tonic cadences in the ordinary (not in the orchestrally accompanied) recitatives of *Griselda* may have been intended to suggest this method of realization. In the present state of our knowledge this whole question must remain open.[5] It may be remarked, incidentally, that there is no need to suppose that the continuo would have been realized in exactly the same way at every dominant–tonic cadence in the recitatives.

There is one other little puzzle in the notation of Scarlatti's recitative: What is the significance of tied bass notes within a measure? There is often no apparent necessity for them; they do not always coincide with a rest in the voice part or with a change of personage, nor do rests or changes invariably coincide with tied notes in the bass. Yet these tied notes are plainly in the autograph and are scrupulously reproduced in the copies. Tentatively, they may be interpreted as a direction or reminder to the cembalist to repeat a chord either literally or in a different position—but this interpretation is by no means certain.

Embellishments

As already mentioned, improvised embellishments were incorporated in varying degree in the written solo vocal lines without any indication being provided in the score. Vocal cadenzas, more or less elaborate and likewise improvised (at least in theory), might be inserted before the final dominant–tonic resolution at the end of one or both parts of a *da capo* aria or at other places. Occasionally a hint of such decorations appears in the score of *Griselda*: the direction "ad arbitrio" in the arias Numbers 17 and 34, the "fermata del Sig. Tenore" in Number 15, and the fermatas in Numbers 9, 24, 49, and elsewhere are probably indications for improvised cadenzas.

5. See Sven H. Hansell, "The Cadence in 18th-century Recitative" in *The Musical Quarterly*, LIV, No. 2 (April 1968): 228–248.

GRISELDA

Cast of Characters

Gualtiero, King of Sicily	Alto
Griselda, Queen, wife of Gualtiero	Soprano
Costanza, Princess, their daughter	Soprano
Ottone, Sicilian Noble	Alto
Corrado, Prince of Puglia	Tenor
Roberto, Younger brother of Corrado	Soprano
Everardo, infant son of Gualtiero and Griselda (non-singing part)	

Scene: Vicinity of Palermo

Changes of Scene

ACT I
Magnificent room, destined for public audiences, with throne
Seaport with ships
Aristocratic antechamber, with entrance to the royal apartments
Royal quarters

ACT II
Countryside with rustic dwelling, grove, hill, and waterfall
Great gallery
Wooded spot with various paths, and sea in the distance. To one
   side, Griselda's hut with rustic bed

ACT III
Royal apartment with small throne
Side-lit avenue in the royal gardens
Amphitheater, decked out with illuminations and other ornamentation

1. Sinfonia avanti l'Opera

16

19

21

ATTO PRIMO

Luogo magnifico destinato per le pubbliche udienze. Dall'un dei lati trono reale
con due sedili. Dall'altro Grandi del Regno, e popoli. Ordini militari in distanza.
Gualtiero, col suo reale accompagnamento, che poi si schiera intorno al trono.

2. Recitativo

Va sul trono

Segue

3. Coro

Griselda con suo equipaggio e i suddetti

4. *Recitativo*

5. *Aria*

30

tro - ve - rò.

Ciò che a te pia - ce, in ciò che bra - mi,

tutti

solo

la___ mia gio - ia_____ e la mia pa - ce___ sem - pre sem - pre, o ca - ro,

ca - ro io tro - ve - rò_____, io tro - ve - rò; gio - ia, pa - ce, ca - ro, ca - ro, ca - ro,

io tro-ve-rò_____, io tro-ve-rò.

tutti

Non mi chie - der che io non t'a - mi, non vie - tar - mi che io t'a-do - ri.

solo

Dim - mi, dim - mi poi: Gri - sel - da mo - ri, mo - ri, che io con - ten - ta, con-ten - ta____

mo - ri - rò_____. Non mi chie-der che io non t'a-mi, non vie-tar-mi che io t'a - do - ri, dim - mi

poi: Gri-sel-da mo - ri, mo - ri, che io con-ten - - - - - ta, con-

ten - ta mo - ri - rò, mo - ri - rò_____, con-ten - ta, con-ten-ta mo-ri-rò.

Da capo

Ottone (che ferma Griselda nel partir) e i medesimi

6. Recitativo

Ottone (a Griselda) Griselda (torna indietro) Gualtiero Ott.

Res-ta, e sa-prai. (Che fia?) Che ar-re-chi, Ot-to-ne? Il Prin-ci-pe Cor-ra-do gia con pro-ra pom-po-sa toc-ca il

Gualt.

por-to vi-ci-no, e a te con-du-ce, co-me im-po-sto gli fu, la re-gia spo-sa. La re-gia spo-sa? Ad-dio, Gri-sel-da! Io

Gris. Gualt. Gris.

par-to. E do-ve? Ad in-con-trar-la. E con tal fret-ta? E con tal gio-ia? O Dio! Sì vi-ci-no e-ra il col-po, che uc-

Gualt. (verso Ottone) Gris.

ci-der-mi do-vea? Dun-que mi la-sci? Dun-que ti per-do? An-dian-ne: at-te-so io so-no. Nè pur

l'ul-ti-mo am-ples-so, nè pur l'ul-ti-mo sguar-do, pria che ad al-tri ti do-ni a me con-ce-di, e al-la sven-tu-ra mia? Trop-po mi

Gris.

chie-di. Dun-que, Gual-tie-ro, ad-di-o. (O spo-so! O re-gno! O Fa-to a-cer-bo e ri-o!)

7. *Aria*

36

che vi - bra-no stra - - - li.

Le_ pu - pil - le che il ren - do-no a - man - te ab - ba - stan - za son lu - ci - de e

bel - le quan - do so - no pu - pil - le re - a - - - - li,

ab - ba - stan-za_ son_ lu - ci- de e bel - le   quan - do   so - no_ pu - pil - le   re-

a - li____, pu-pil - le   re-

a - - - - - li.

Dal segno

Griselda e Ottone

8. Recitativo

Ottone: Re-gi-na, se più ba-di, più Re-gi-na non se - i.

Griselda: (Quan-to im-por-tu - no mi fu sem-pre co-stu - i!)

Ott.: Dal-le tue tem-pia ca-de già la co-ro-na; a ser-bar-te-la Ot-to-ne è sol ba-stan-te, fi - do vas-sal-lo e ca-va-lie-re a-man-te.

Gris.: Chi mi to-glie il dia-de-ma, un suo do-no mi to-glie; e al-lor che io la-scio le in-se-gne di Re - gi-na, il cor ne ser-bo.

Ott.: Io, se tu me l'im-po-ni, fre-ne-rò la bal-dan-za del vol-go au-da-ce, as-sa-li-rò la reg-gia, tur-be-rò di Gual-tie-ro i vi-ci-ni spon-sa-li, sve-ne-rò chi ti to-glie il no-me di Re-gi-na e

quel di mo-glie. I - ni-quo!, e l'o-se-re-sti? E a me ne chie-di, te-me-

ra-rio, l'as-sen-so? E tal, e tal mi cre-di? Pen-sa, pen-sa quan-to ti

co-sta un in-giu-sto ri-pu-dio, e quan-to per-di ri-fiu - tan-do il fa-vor del-la mia spa - da.

Al fin che per-do? Il re-gno. Non e-ra mi - o. Lo spo-so. Me-co lo por-to. Il

fi-glio. Na-cque al suo ge-ni-to - re. Un ca - ro sguar-do, u - na dol-ce spe-ran - za che tu mi do - ni,

i - do-lo mio, ti giu-ro... Del tuo fa-vor non cu-ro, le tue bra-me de-te-sto, o - dio il tuo a-mo - re;

a prez-zo d'u-na col-pa non am-bi-sco un im-pe-ro. An-drò con-ten-ta o-ve il ciel mi de-

sti - na: Fin-che il sen-so è vas-sal-lo, io son Re-gi-na.

Attacca subito l'Aria

40

9. Aria

Nel-l'a - - - - - spro mio do-lor no, no, non ti lu-sin-ghi, non ti lu-

sin-ghi il cor va-na spe-ran - za, va - - - - - na spe-ran - za.

Nel-l'a-spro mio do - lor non ti lu-sin-ghi il_ cor va-na spe-ran - za,

41

va - - - - na spe-ran - za, il cor non ti lu - sin-ghi, non ti lu - sin-ghi, no!,

Cadenza

tutti

va - na, va - - na spe-ran - za. Ve-

drai che io son più for - te del - la cru-del mia sor - te, ve-drai, ve-drai che a-mor mi die - de per a - ni - ma la

solo

Scena v

Ottone

10. *Recitativo*

Trop-po av-vez-za è Gri-sel-da tra le por-por-e e il fa-sto, per non es-ser-mi cru-da. El-la il co-man-do non an-co-ra de-po-se, e la co-ro-na a-di-to an-cor non la-scia ai miei so-spi-ri. Ma lon-ta-na dal so-glio, a-vrà for-se pie-tà del mio cor-do-glio.

11. *Aria*

Allegro

Violino I, II

Viola

Ottone

Continuo

Chi Re-gi-na mi di-sprez-za, pa-sto-rel-la, pa-sto-rel-la m'a-me-rà, m'a-me-rà.

Chi Re-gi-na

44

mi di - sprez - za,   mi di - sprez - za,   pa - sto - rel - la,   pa - sto - rel - la

m'a - me - rà,   m'a - me - rà _____

_____ ,   pa - sto - rel - la m'a - me - rà _____ ,

m'a - me - rà.

45

Da capo

46

Scena vi

Porto di mare vicino alla città. Navi che veleggiano in lontananza. Approda ricco naviglio
dal quale sbarcano, con seguito di cavalieri, donzelle e guardie, Corrado, Roberto e Costanza.

12. Sinfonia

per lo sbarco. I due corni da caccia staranno sulla nave.

Si fa tutta [di] seguito, senza repliche

47

13. *Aria*

de - le, cru - de - le il mio fa - to mi vol - le gui - dar_____

_____, mi vol - le gui - dar_____, mi

vol - le gui - dar.

tutti

Co - me pre - sto, pre - sto,

pre - sto_ nel_ por - to_ cru - de - le il mio fa - to mi_ vol - le gui - dar_____

solo

mi vol - le gui - dar, mi vol - le___ gui - dar___

52

mi vol - le, mi vol - le gui-

dar.

Quan - do al-

tutti

53

tro - ve le stan - che mie ve - le nem - bo i - ra - to do - ve - va por - tar,   quan - do al -

tro - ve le stan - che mie ve - le nem - bo i - ra - to do - ve - va por - tar,

54

nem - bo i - ra - - - - - - - - - - - -
solo

- - - - - - - - - - to_____ do - ve - va, do - ve - va por - tar.

Da capo

55

14. Recitativo

15. *Aria*

ra.   Chi sa?   Chi sa?

Seb-be - ne il Fa-to si mo-stra i - ra - to,   non pos - so cre-de-re___ che vo-glia of-fen-de - re_____ col suo ri-

go - re___ tan - ta bel - tà.   Chi sa?   Chi sa? Non pos-so cre-de-re, no,   che il Fa-to__ vo-glia, vo-glia of-

fen-de-re tan-ta   bel - tà_____   , tan - ta__ bel-tà. Chi sa? Chi sa?__

Da capo

16. Recitativo

Ec - co il por - to, ec - co il li - do sì fu - ne - sto per me, per te sì lie - to.

Que - sta che pre - mi, o bel - la, è la Si - ci - lia; e quel - la è l'al - ta reg - gia, o - ve Gual - tie - ro at -

ten - de leg - gi dal ci - glio tuo per dar - le ai re - gni. Ah Ro - ber - to, Ro - ber - to! Tu so -

spi - ri, ed ac - co - gli me - sta le tue gran - dez - ze? Quan - to più vo - len - tie - ri mi sce - lie - rei vi - ver pri -

va - ta, e lun - gi da quel - la reg - gia in cui mi sa - rà sem - pre o - gni gran - dez - za a - ma - ra,

pur - chè io di te, tu di me fos - si. (O ca - ra!) Un so - lo de' tuoi sguar - di vin - ce di pre - gio

o - gni re - al for - tu - na. Ep - pur quan - do la lu - ce del - l'au - reo scet - tro e del ver - mi - glio am -

man-to ti ve-drai ba-le-nar sul-le pu-pil-le, ti sem-bre-rà che o-scu-ro sia quell' ar-dor che o-ra per me t'ac-

cen-de, e in pen-san-do che por-ti co-ro-na-te le chio-me, sprez-ze-rai di Ro-ber-to an-co-ra il no-me.

Cost. Mal co-no-sci il mio co-re, ep-pur tut-to, tut-to il pos-sie-di. An-dian-ne o-ra, se il chie-di, o-

ve è me-no di ri-schio e più di pa-ce; se-gui-rò, se-gui-rò l'or-me tue do-ve ti pia-ce. *Rob.* No, no!

Re-gna nel mon-do co-me nell' al-ma mia. Si vil non so-no, che a di-scen-der dal tro-no io ti sor-

Cost. tas-si, non t'a-me-rei, se a prez-zo tal ti a-mas-si. Pen-sa, che se io m'u-ni-sco ad al-tro spo-so

tu dal mio fian-co e dal mio cor do-vrai per sem-pre al-lon-ta-nar-ti ed a me vie-te-ran-no an-che il mi-rar-ti, per tuo, per mio ca-

Rob. sti-go, o-no-re e fe-de. Lo so; ma pur de-sio più la gran-dez-za tua che il pia-cer mio.

60

17. *Aria*

pro - ve - rai ____, che pe - - na pro - ve - rai per - den - - - do u - na bel - tà che t'a - ma

tan - to, tan - to, tan - to, che t'a - ma tan - - to, che, che t'a - ma tan -

Cadenza

to. Se di al - tri me ve-

tutti

solo

drai, al - lo - ra pian - ge - rai, se di al - tri me ve - drai, pian - ge - rai, pian - ge - rai, ma, ma va - no al-

lor sa - rà stil - lar - si in pian - to, stil - lar - si in pian - to; ma va - no al - lor sa-

rà stil - lar - si in pian - to, stil - lar - si in pian - to_____. Bel lab - bro,

ad arbitrio

tutti   colla voce

Dal segno

63

Gualtiero con numeroso corteggio. Ottone, Corrado, Roberto, e poi Costanza.

18. *Recitativo*

cer, fi-gli d'A-mo-re! Si-gnor, l'al-ma sor-pre-sa dal-le gra-zie re-a-li col si-len-zio ri-spon-de, e al-lor che ta-ce

ne' suoi ti-mi-di af-fet-ti è più lo-qua-ce. (Sof-fri, o mi-se-ro cor!) (Me-sto è il ger-ma-no.) Vie-ni, vie-ni o-mai, mia di-let-ta, vie-ni me-co a go-

der par-te d'un so-glio, che il Ciel ti pre-pa-rò fin dal-la cu-na. Tu pur ver-rai, Ro-ber-to, o di cep-po re-al

ger-me ben de-gno; og-gi da voi ri-ce-va or-na-men-to la reg-gia e gio-ia il re-gno. Gran Re, trop-po, trop-po mi o-

no-ri. Ot-to-ne! In-cli-to Si-re. Se non u-scì Gri-sel-da da-gli al-ber-ghi re-a-li fa che n'e-sca a mo-men-ti, on-de in-

ciam-po non re-chi a miei con-ten-ti. E-se-gui-sco il co-man-do. Ma tu me-sta mi sem-bri, ti-mi-det-ta non par-li, e con le

mie non s'in-con-tra-no mai le tue pu-pil-le. Di te-ne-ra fan-ciul-la al ver-gi-nal ros-so-re do-na, o Si-gnor, l'in-vo-lon-ta-rio er-

ro-re. Fin-chè la bel-la i suoi ti-mo-ri af-fi-da da voi non si di-vi-da, scor-ge-te-la al-la reg-gia.

Tu Ro-ber-to l'as-si-sti, e tu Cor-ra-do dil-le, co-me ben sai, che pri-ma di ve-der-la an-cor l'a-ma-i.

19. Aria

66

glia, co - me spo - sa e co - me fi - glia, e co - me fi - glia io ti ven - go ad ab - brac-ciar, ad ab - brac - ciar non te - mer, no, co-me spo - sa e co-me fi - glia, co - me fi - glia, ti ven - go ad ab - brac - ciar.

Da capo

Corrado, Roberto, Costanza e loro seguito.

20. *Recitativo*

21. *Aria*

giac-chè la mia gran - dez - za è tua fe - li - ci - tà

è tua fe - li - ci - tà, fe - li - ci - tà, fe - li - ci - tà.

Bell' al - ma go - di, go - di ral - le - gra - ti, go - di con - so - la - ti,

giac-chè la mia gran - dez - za è tua fe - li - ci - tà, è tua fe - li - ci -

tà

è tua fe - li - ci - tà, fe - li - ci - ta,

Cadenza

è tua fe - li - ci - tà.

Re -

gi - na mi__ vo - le - sti, re - gi - na mi__ fa - ce - sti; il

Cie - lo del__ tuo ze - lo mer - cè __, mer - cè __ ti ren - de - rà.

Re - gi - na mi vo - le - sti, re - gi - na mi fa - ce - sti, il Cie - lo

del tuo ze - lo mer - cè __, mer - cè ti__ ren - de - rà __

__, mer - cè __ ti ren - de - rà.

Dal segno

Scena x
Corrado e Roberto.

22. *Recitativo*

Roberto

Ah Cor - ra - do, ah ger - ma - no, se la bel - la Co - stan - za es - ser mia non do - vea, es - ser mia non po - tea, per - chè, per - chè fin da pri - mi an - ni non vie - tar - mi d'a - mar - la? Per - che a - du - lar co - sì le mie spe - ran - ze? Per - chè, per - chè tra - di - re i vo - ti miei? Cru - de - le! So ben che pian - ge - re - sti l'in - gan - no tuo se tu ve - de - sti, o Dio! lo stra - zio del cor mi - o.

Corrado

Ro - ber - to, i no - stri e - ven - ti na - sco - no in Ciel pri - ma che in ter - ra, e a noi pre - ve - der - li è vie - ta - to. Ma pu - re av - vien che i be - ni spes - so di ma - le han - no sem - bian - za. Im - pe - ra al tuo do - lor nè t'at - tri - star co - tan - to, e pen - sa che ta - lo - ra ad un ve - ro gio - ir fa stra - da il pian - to.

Scena xi
Roberto.

23. *Recitativo*

Roberto

Quai fo - le? Quai lu - sin - ghe? O - mai sì chia - ra è la per - di - ta mia che il du - bi - tar - ne sa - reb - be va - ni - ta di men - te in - sa - na. Pur - trop - po al re - gio sguar - do pia - cque la mia vez - zo - sa. E chi, e chi può mai ve - de - re e non a - mar sì va - ghi rai?

73

24. Aria

nar _____, per non pe - nar   co -

sì.   Non vi __ vor - rei co - no - sce - re, be -

gli oc - chi lu - sin - ghie - ri,   be - gli oc - chi __ lu - sin - ghie - ri,   per non __   pe - nar _____

per non pe - nar co - sì, per non pe - nar

per non pe - nar co - sì.

tutti

Cadenza

Ma giac-chè pe-no tan-to non vi mo-stra-te al - te - ri, non

solo

Atrio nobile con ingresso agli appartamenti reali, che si vedono in distanza.
Griselda in abito di pastorella, esclusa sulla soglia da alcune guardie.

25. *Recitativo*

Scena xiii
Griselda e Gualtiero con seguito.

26. *Recitativo*

ce-ver l'e-stre-mo, sia pie-to-so, o cru-del, sem - pre tuo sguar-do. Che? Di te mi fa-vel-li? Ed io cre-dea

che la nuo-va mia spo-sa t'oc-cu-pas-se il pen-sier. La vi-di, la vi-di, o quan-to va-ga e gen-til! Tu

stes-sa l'a-me-re-sti, o Gri-sel-da. E l'a-mo, e l'a-mo an-ch'io; ciò che pia-ce al tuo af-fet-to è ca-ro al mi-o.

Vo' che tu ve-da il dar-do on-de ho tra-fit-to dol-ce-men-te il cuo-re. Qui lo va-gheg-gia. (O cie-li! Qual i-

ma-go! Qual vol-to!) Che ti sem-bra? Ah Si-gno-re, ne' suoi lu-mi hai tuoi lu-mi, nel-la sua la tua fron-te, e in lei rav-vi-so

so-lo al-quan-to men ri - gi-do il tuo vi-so. È bel-la? È di te de-gna. Go - drò, go-drò se-co-lo fe-li - ce.

Il Ciel ti dia con sì dol - ce com-pa-gna lun-ga e-tà, fau-sto im-pe-ro; de' tuoi fi-gli i ni-po-ti ti scher-zi-no d'in-tor-no,

e ap-pe-na in tan-ta se-rie d'al-te for-tu - ne ti sov-ven-ga ta-lo-ra del-la mi-se-ra tua fi-da Gri-sel-da.

Non più, non più! Par-to, par-to mio Si - re, lun - gi dal ca-ro og-get - to trop-po qui ti rat-ten-ni la for - za che ti

fai, ti mi-ro in fron-te. Tor-na, tor-na ai bo-schi e t'af-fret-ta, che io tor-no a va-gheg-giar la mia di-let-ta.

27. Aria

80

bel - la ti - ran - nia, che dol - ce, dol-ce in-can - to tro - vò que - sto mio co-re, que - sto mio

co - re in due pu - pil - le, bel - la ti - ran-ni - a, dol - ce in - can - - - -

to in due pu - pil - le!

tutti

Griselda, alla quale vien condotto Everardo suo figlio; poi Ottone.

28. *Recitativo*

29. Aria

cò, non si pla-cò. Di', se mai me-no sde-gno-sa lo sguar-do gi-ro, di', di', che è l'i-ra in pet-to a-sco-sa ma non

già _____ che si pla-cò, no, no, non già che si pla-co, non già, no, no.

Da capo

Scena xv

Ottone con Everardo, che poi è ricondotto altrove.

30. *Recitativo*

Ottone

Con bel-tà sì pro-ter-va, so-no i-nu-ti-li sfor-zi i prie-ghi, e i vez-zi. Al-tra

via ten-te-rò, già la di-seg-no. Si u-si l'ar-te e l'in-ge-gno, chè sen-za qual-che

fro-de chi è sprez-za-to in a-mor giam-mai, giam-mai non go-de.

31. *Aria*

Vor- rei pla - car - la, ma non so

poi se gli oc-chi suoi sa-ran sì bel - li quan - do è pla - ca - ta____ quan-do è pla - ca - ta____, ma

90

non so, non so se gli oc-chi suoi sa-ran sì bel - li quan-do è pla - ca - ta, quan-do è pla - ca -

ta.

tutti

Dal segno

91

Scena xvi
Quarto reale nobilamente preparato per Costanza.
Tavolino a parte con manto, scettro e corona.
Corrado e Costanza.

32. *Recitativo*

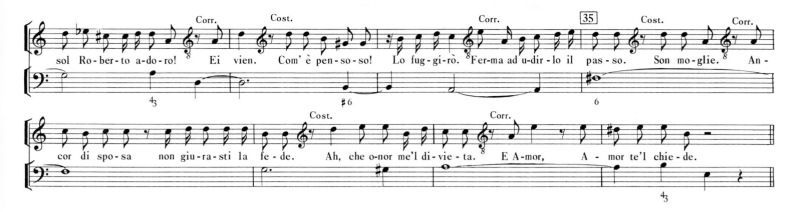

sol Ro-ber-to a-do-ro! Ei vien. Com' è pen-so-so! Lo fug-gi-rò. Fer-ma ad u-dir-lo il pas-so. Son mo-glie. An-cor di spo-sa non giu-ra-sti la fe-de. Ah, che o-nor me'l vie-ta. E A-mor, A-mor te'l chie-de.

Scena xvii

Costanza, e poi Roberto.

33. Recitativo

Pria che d'a-mar-ti io la-sci la vi-ta la-sce-ro, dol-ce mio be-ne; ma qui gio-vi al-le mie, al fin-ger cru-del-tà per le sue pe-ne. Co-stan-za! Ahi-mè, che veg-gio? Ti al-lon-ta-ni mi fug-gi e ta-ci? E mi con-ten-di an-che di un guar-do il mi-se-ro di-let-to? Sde-gna a-mo-re il mio gra-do, e vuol ri-spet-to. (Cor mio, non v'è più spe-me.) U-di-sti? U-dii, Re-gi-na. Or, che bra-mi? Al tuo pie-de in-chi-nar-mi un mo-men-to e fa-vel-lar-ti. Al-tro? Non più. Ri-spet-ta il gra-do e par-ti. Ub-bi-di-rò, ma pria dim-mi con qual co-rag-gio o con qual ar-te hai già po-sto in o-blio.. Re-gi-na e mo-glie, ben il ve-di o Ro-ber-to al-tri a-scol-tar non deg-gio, al-tri non deg-gio a-mar, che il Re mio spo-so. Ah Ro-ber-to in fe-li-ce! (Fos-se al-me-no Gual-tier co-sì vez-zo-so!)

93

34. *Aria*

94

te bel-lez - ze, bel-lez-ze a-ma - te; lo so _, lo ve-do e, e ne ho pie - tà _, ne ho pie-tà, pie -

tà _, pie - tà _, lo ve - do, lo so, lo so, e ne ho pie - tà.

Ma trop - po, o Dio! so - spi - ro anch'io per _ non ar -

mar-mi di cru-del-tà __, di cru-del - tà. Ma trop-po, trop-po, o Dio! so - spi -ro, so-spi-ro anch'io, per

non ar-mar — — — — — — — — — mi, so-spi - ro, so-spi -

ro per non ar - mar - mi di cru-del - tà. Voi,

tutti

Dal segno

96

35. *Recitativo*

Chi, chi vi-de mai de-sti-no e-gual-le al mio? Fin tra le brac-cia A - mo-re mi get-tò la mia bel - la.

Quan-do io già qua-si la strin-ge-va e qua-si ne go - de-va il pos-ses-so in un ba - le-no me la ra - pì, me la sbal-

zò dal se - no. Nel mio pen-o-so af-fan-no la per - di-ta m'af-flig-ge, e più l'in-gan - no.

36. *Aria*

A-man - ti, a-man - ti che_ pian-ge-te _, che_ pian-ge -

le la-gri-me ter - ge-te, le la-gri-me ter - ge-te e con-so-la - - - - - - - - - - - - - - - - - - te-vi_____, e con-so-la - te-vi.

A-man - ti che pian-ge-te, le la-gri-me ter-

98

ge-te, le_ la-gri-me ter-ge-te e con-so-la - - - - - - - - -

- te-vi, e con-so-la - te-vi, e con-so-la - - - - - -

- - - - - - - - - - - - - - - - - - - te-vi,

Cadenza

e con-so-la - te-vi.

tutti

Per tut - ti i co - ri a - man - ti io so - lo, so - lo pe - ne - rò, io

solo

so - lo pian-ge - rò, voi ral - le - gra - - - - - te-vi.

tutti

Io so - lo, so - lo per tut - ti, per tut - ti pe - ne - rò, per tut - ti_ pian-ge - rò,
solo

voi ral - le - gra - - - - - - - - - - - - - - - - - - - te - vi, voi ral-le - gra - - te - vi.

Da capo

Fine del Atto Primo

ATTO SECONDO

Campagna con abitazione rusticale, boschetto, collina, e caduta d'acqua.
Griselda.

37. *Aria*

Mi ri - ve - di o sel - va om-bro - sa, ma non più Re-gi -na e spo - sa, mi ri-

ve - di sven-tu-ra - ta, mi ri - ve-di sven - tu-ra - ta, di-sprez-za-ta, di-sprez-za-ta pa-sto-rel - la, sven-tu-

ra - ta, di-sprez-za - - ta pa-sto-rel - la.

È pur quel - lo, quel - lo, quel - lo il pa - trio mon - te, que-sta è pur l'a - mi - ca

fon - te, quel-lo è il pra - to e il que-sto è il ri - o; e sol i - o, e sol io non son, no, no, non son più quel -

la no, non son più quel-la no, non son più, no, non son più quel - la _____. Mi ri -

Dal segno

Ottone e Griselda.

38. *Recitativo*

39. Aria

lom - ba in - na - mo - ra - - ta dal ca - ro a - man - te a - ma - ta non o - dia il suo fe - de - le non

è con lui cru - de - le, ma di - ce in sua fa - vel - la: a - - ma chi t'a - ma_____. Co-

109

lom - ba in-na - mo - ra - ta non o - dia il suo fe - de - le, ma di - ce in sua fa - vel - la: a -

- - - - ma, a - ma chi t'a - ma; a - ma di - ce, a - ma chi

t'a - ma, a - - - - - - - ma, a - ma chi t'a -

ma.   Ren-di tu pu-re, tu pu-re o bel - la, a-mo-re per a-mo-re   e

do-na il tuo bel co - re a chi_____, a chi ti bra - - ma,   e do-na il tuo bel

co - re a chi,   a chi ti bra - - - ma_____, a chi ti bra - - - ma.

Da capo

111

40. *Recitativo*

Ho in pet-to u-na sol al-ma, ho so-lo un co-re, e que-sto di Gual-tie-ro sa-

rà fin-chè io re-spi-ri. Bel-la in-fe-li-ce, ar-re-sta il pas-so e mi-ra il

do-no che io ti por-to. O fi-glio! O do-no! Di cru-do im-pe-ro

e-se-cu-tor qui so-no. Cie-li, che sa-rà mai? Do-ve più fol-ti spar-ge il

bo-sco gli or-ro-ri de-vo e-spor-re al-le fie-re il tuo E-ve-rar-do. Hai più stra-li o For-tu-na da vi-

brar sul mio ca-po? E tu, e tu cru-de-le, con sì bel do-no a me ve-ni-sti? Leg-gi,

leg-gi o ma-gna-ni-ma don-na, nel mio sem-bian-te il mio do-lor, ma è for-za che s'a-dem-pia il co-man-do.

41. *Aria*

114

va u - na stel - la.

A - gi - ta - ta da fie - ra pro - cel - la lan - gui -

- va, lan - gui - va u - na ro - sa che pom - po - sa tra le ro - se

115

sem - bra - - - - - - va u - na stel - la, sem - bra - -

- - va u - na stel - la.

116

la - va più al - te - ra e più bel - la, più al - te - - - - - - - - - - - - - ra e più bel - la, più bel - - - - - - - - - ra e più bel - la, più bel - la. A - gi -

Dal segno

Scena iv

Griselda con Everardo, poi Ottone, con ferro nudo, e seguaci.

42. *Recitativo*

43. *Aria*

Qui guarda il figlio,
poi dice irata ad Ottone

Che far pos-s'i-o? Ti-ran - - no, ti-ran - no! L'a-

tutti con cembalo

solo

mor di ma-dre a-man-te mi squar-cia, mi squar-cia in pet-to, mi squar-cia in pet-to il cor, il cor, ma il cor trop-po co-stan-te

co-sì squar-cia-to an-cor, co-sì squar-cia-to an-cor vin-ce, vin-ce, vin-ce il suo af-fan - - no, vin-ce il suo af-fan - no.

Da capo

122

44. Recitativo

45. Aria

Gran galleria. Roberto e Costanza.

46. *Recitativo*

rez-za o con men di fie-rez-za, in-vo-lan-do al tuo spo-so e do-nan-do al mio duo-lo un vez-zo,

u-na lu-sin-ga, un so-spir so-lo. Co-sì... Che-ta-ti, in-gra-to; non me-ri-

ti pie-tà. Ve-di, che pos-so anch' io sde-gnar-mi. E poi? Sa-prò, sa-prò se

vo-glio ren-der fa-sto per fa-sto, or-go-glio per or-go-glio, di-sprez-zo per di-sprez-zo, e ven-di-

car-mi. Che? Pen-si di la-sciar-mi? E tu che pen-si, che io non pos-sa do-nar gli af-

fet-ti miei a bel-tà più gen-ti-le e for-se an-co-ra fi-da, e co-stan-te più di te? Spie-

ta-to, po-tre-sti far-lo? E tu, e tu no'l fai? Tan-to ol-tre il do-

lor ti tra-spor-ta? Il do-lo-re e l'a-mor. Va, va, non m'im-por-ta.

attacca subito

127

47. Aria

Tu, tu non in-ten-di, no, non in-ten-di, che pe-na si-a la ge-lo-si-a, la ge-lo-si-a per-chè, per-chè t'a-do---ro con fe-del-tà___, con fe-del-tà.

128

No no___, tu non in - ten-di che___ pe-na___ si - a la___ ge-lo-si - a per -

chè, per-chè t'a-do-ro, t'a-do-ro, t'a-do - - - ro con fe-del - tà, con

fe-del - tà_____, con fe-del - tà.

Ma for-se, for-se, ma for-se al-lo-ra l'in-ten-de-rai, l'in-ten-de-rai quan-do ve-dra-i, quan-do ve-drai che un'al-tra

bel - la_____, un'al-tra bel - la mi pia-ce-rà, l'in-ten-de - rai quan-do ve - drai che un'al-tra bel-la,

bel - la, bel - la, bel - - la mi pia-ce - rà, mi pia - ce - rà.

Da capo
Nel partire Roberto s'incontra con Gualtiero,
che lo prende per mano e lo riconduce a Costanza.

130

48. *Recitativo*

49. Aria

Lu - ce mia bel - la, non sei con - ten - ta no, non sei con - ten - ta, ve - do ben io, ve - do ben io che ti tor - men - ta, che ti _____ tor - men - ta _____, che ti tor - men - ta un non so che, un non so che.

* Gli Oubuoè... attaccono al Segno *, e lasciano al Segno □ [*Santini, f. 9*]

132

50. *Recitativo*

Sa-rai pa-go, o Ro-ber-to: le tue bra-me a-dem-pi-te og-gi ve-drai, og-gi Gual-tier... Che

fai? Che la-gri-me son que-ste? Il tuo gran co-re che in-tre-pi-do vo-lea le mie gran-dez-ze, dov' è? dov'

è? Co-sì, co-sì ti can-gi? Non mi per-de-sti an-co-ra, e tu, e tu mi pian-gi?

51. *Aria*

Se di al-tri, se di al-tri io ti de-si-o bel-lis-si-mo i-dol

mi - o, non ti sde-gnar, non ti sde-gnar con me ma, ma, ma con A-mo - re, con A-mo - re.

No, non ti sde-gnar, se di al-tri ti de-sio, bel-lis-si-mo i-dol mio non ti sde-gnar con

me, ma, ma con A-mo-re, con A-mo - re no, no, no, con me no, non ti sde-gnar_____, ma, ma con A-

52. *Recitativo*

Sì, sì, con A-mor mi sde-gno, con A-mor che tra-di-sce co-sì bel-le spe-ran-ze, con A-

mor che sì cru-da em-pia mer-ce-de ren-de a tan-ti so-spi-ri e a tan-ta fe-de.

53. *Aria*

Grave e staccato

Qua-lor ti-ran-no A-mo-re tra

solo

lac - - - - - ci pren-de un co-re, l'al-let-ta e lo lu-sin-ga e

scem-pio poi ne fa_____, e scem - - pio poi ne fa.

A-mo-re pren-de, pren-de un co-re tra lac - - - - - - - - ci, l'al-let - - - - - - - ta e lo lu-sin - -

ga, ma scem-pio poi ne fa_____, e scem-pio

poi ne fa.

tutti

Tal va-go par-go-let-to se pren_____de un au-gel-

solo

140

let - to, scher-zan - do l'ac-ca-rez - za e mor - te poi gli dà, mor - te poi _____

_____ gli dà, scher - zan - do l'ac-ca-rez _ _ _ _ _ _ _ _

- za _____ e mor - te poi gli dà _____, mor - te poi gli dà.

Da capo

Parte di selva con viali diversi, e mare in lontananza.
In disparte capanna pastorale di Griselda, che vedesi aperta
con letto rustico nel mezzo, ed altre capanne contigue..
Griselda.

54. *Recitativo*

E de-li-quio di co - re o stan-chez-za di pian - to quel - la che o - ra vi op-pri - me, o mie pu-pil - le?

Son - no non è, chè voi l'u - so più non a - ve - te di pla - ci-da qui - e - te; ma quan-do pur sia son-no che

de' miei ma - li a scher-no vo - glia far - mi po-sar sia son - no, sia son - no e-ter - no.

55. *Aria*

Andante moderato

Flauti I, II

Violino I

Violino II

Viola

Griselda

Fi-ni-

Continuo

Del-la pro-le e del con-sor-te e del

Re-gno mi spo-glie-sti sol la vi-ta mi la-scia-sti e pur que-sta, e pur que-sta io ti da-rò, mi la-scia-sti la vi-ta, la vi-ta

sol, e pur que-sta, e pur que-sta io ti da-rò.

tutti

Fi-ni-

Dal segno

Dopo l'aria Griselda s'addormenta. Segue intanto la caccia reale,
e si vedono attraversar la scena cervi, daini, ed altri animali selvaggi
(che in detto luogo ve n'è abbondanza) inseguiti da cacciatori del Re,
armati di dardi. E si suona la seguente Sinfonia.

144

56. Sinfonia

Si fa seguito senza mai tornar da capo

145

Griselda addormenta nella capanna.
Costanza e Roberto

57. *Recitativo*

58. *Aria*

pu - pil - le a - ma - te. Se a - pri - te

tutti   solo

tan - te pia - ghe quan - do vi ve - do i - ra - te, quan - te sa - ran - no al - lor se vi pla - ca -

- te, vi pla - ca - te, quan - te sa - ran - no al - lor se vi pla - ca - te, vi___ pla - ca - te?

Da capo

150

Costanza, e Griselda che dorme

59. *Recitativo*

60. Duetto

153

quel -la, che quel-la se - i.

No_____ non sei quel -la ep - pu-re il

quel -la, che quel-la se - i.

No_____ non sei quel -la ep - pu-re il

tutti   solo

\#   \#   \#   \#6   6   \#6 3
                             4

co - re   di-ce al co - re,   di-ce al cor   che quel-la,   che quel-la se - i,   pur di-ce il cor_____

co - re   di-ce al co - re,   di-ce al cor   che quel-la, quel-la se - i,   pur di-ce il cor_____

che quel-la se - i, che, che quel-la se - i.

che quel-la se - i, che, che quel-la se - i.

tutti

Ca - re lab-bra, ca - re lab-bra in voi ri -

Va - ghe lu - ci, va - ghe

solo

mi - ro, ri - mi - ro quel - la fi - glia, quel - la fi - glia che per - de - i, in voi ri - mi - ro

lu - ci in voi ri - mi - ro quel - la ma - dre che so - spi - ro,

in voi ri -

quel - la fi - glia, fi - glia che per - de - i, che, che per - de - i. Non sei

mi - ro quel - la ma - dre, ma - dre che so - spi - ro, che, che so - spi - ro. Non sei

tutti

Dal segno

156

61. *Recitativo*

Corrado con seguito e detti

62. *Recitativo*

63. *Aria*

159

161

Griselda, poi Ottone

64. *Recitativo*

Va a prendere il suo dardo
lasciato sul letto

Griselda: Ec-co Ot-ton. So-la, i-ner-me, che far pos-so? Il mio dar-do sia al-men la mia di-fe-sa.

Ottone: Da chi t'a-do-ra ti di-fen-di, o bel-la?

Gris.: Vie-ni pur, vie-ni pur, vie-ni i-ni-quo a sve-nar do-po il fi-glio an-che la ma-dre.

Ott.: A-mo, a-mo E-ve-rar-do e l'a-me-rò qual pa-dre.

Gris.: Ei dun-que vi-ve?

Ott.: E se-co tu pur vi-vrai, Gri-sel-da, e mia vi-vrai, se-gui-mi.

Gris.: Non t'a-scol-to. Ott.: Vie-ni. Gris.: Ver-rei piut-to-sto mil-le vol-te al-la tom-ba.

Ott.: E che far pen-si?. Gris.: Quan-to può un' al-ma di-spe-ra-ta e for-te, dar-ti o ri-ce-ver mor-te.

Ott.: O-là, miei fi-di!

Escono armati

Gris.: Ahi-mè! Soc-cor-so, a-i-ta! Ott.: Trag-ga-si o-ve già dis-si, il Re l'im-po-ne.

162

Gualtiero con le sue guardie, Corrado, Costanza e detti.

65. *Recitativo*

66. *Recitativo*

67. *Trio*

165

a Gualtiero a Costanza

Ed io sem-pre fe - de - le e vi - ve-re e mo - ri - re, mo - ri - re per te, per

mar.

a Gualtiero

te, per te____ sa - prò, per te____ sa - prò.

A-mar ti vo - glio sem-pre

O-diar ti vo - glio sem-pre sem-pre,

tutti   solo

del _____, mo - rir fe - del _____, fe-del mo - rir sa - prò, mo - rir sa - prò.

a - mar _____, a - mar _____, a - mar sa - prò, a - mar sa - prò.

o - diar _____, o - diar _____, o - diar sa - prò, o - diar sa - prò.

a Gualt.

solo

tutti

a Griselda

Sa -

a Cost. a Gualt.

te sa - rò, sem-pre a-mo-ro - sa per te, per te sem-pre a-mo - ro -

sem-pre pie - to - sa, pie - to - sa sa - rò.

sem-pre cru - de - le sa - rò.

sa per te, per te sa - rò.

Ti vo - glio

solo   tutti

Dal segno

Fine del Atto Secondo

170

ATTO TERZO

Gabinetti reali con piccolo trono.
Griselda e Ottone, con Guardie

68. *Recitativo*

Per-fi-do, io ti vo-lea do-ve sei giun-to. Ve-drò, ve-drò pu-ni-ta al fi-ne la tua te-me-ri-tà con la tua mor-te. Tan-ta fie-rez-za in sì bel se-no? I-ni-quo, ti vo-glio e-stin-to. In sì leg-gia-dra boc-ca tan-ta se-te di san-gue? I tuoi de-lit-ti... I miei de-lit-ti, o bel-la, al-tro non son che un gran-de a-mo-re, er-rai, er-rai sol per-chè t'a-mo e per-chè t'a-mo as-sai. Chia-mi ec-ces-si d'a-mor le vi-o-len-ze i tra-di-men-ti e le ra-pi-ne, in-de-gno? Pla-ca il te-ne-ro sde-gno nel-la tu-a bel-lez-za ri-co-no-sci l'au-tor d'o-gni mia col-pa, io sa-rei più in-no-cen-te se tu fos-si men bel-la e più cle-men-te. Ma che fa-ce-sti, o cru-do, del fi-glio mio? Do-v'è, do-v'è? Lo tru-ci-da-sti? Io tru-ci-dar sì ca-ro pe-gno? E co-me? Coi ba-ci for-se? Al ge-ni-tor che l'a-ma al ge-ni-tor che lo so-spi-ra e chie-de pur or lo ren-de il mio fe-de-le A-ra-spe. Se men-ti.... La men-zo-gna pa-ghe-rò con la vi-ta. Ot-to-ne ad-dio, ho pie-tà de' tuoi ma-li. E del mio a-mo-re? Tu sai che pe-no anch'io e che vi-vo senz'al-ma e sen-za co-re.

69. Aria

174

te che io mo - - - - ra? Si va - da, si va - da a mo - rir.

Ma in-tan - to che par - to, ma in-tan - to che mo - ro bei

lu - mi a-mo - ro - si, vol-ge-te - mi un guar-do, bei lab - bri vez-zo-si, vez-

zo-si, get-ta-te un so-spir, un guar-do, bei lu - mi bei lab - - bri, get-

ta-te un so-spir, un so - spir. V'in-

Dal segno

70. *Recitativo*

Costanza: Vieni e strin-gi-mi al pet-to dol-ce com-pa-gna mi-a, do-po il mio spo-so tu sei di que-sto co-re il più te-ne-ro a-mo-re.

Griselda: E tu sei, mia di-let-ta, l'u-ni-co ben che il Fa-to in tan-ti ma-li miei pur m'ha la-scia-to.

Cost.: Co-me t'af-flig-gi, o ca-ra, in ve-der che io ti tol-go ben-chè sen-za mia col-pa il tuo con-sor-te, è per for-za fa-ta-le quan-do me-no il vor-rei ti son ri-va-le?

Gris.: Go-do, o bel-la, co-sì del-la tua sor-te che non pen-so al-la mi-a.

Cost.: For-se la ge-lo-sia un dì col suo ve-le-no la pa-ce tur-be-rà del tuo bel se-no.

Gris.: Il mio mag-gior con-ten-to è che t'a-mi Gual-tie-ro e che tu l'a-mi, e ben più go-de-rò se l'a-me-rai quan-to io stes-so l'a-mai.

Cost.: Che di-re-sti, o mia fi-da? Se io l'a-mi o no, non ben in-ten-do an-co-ra.

Gris.: La tua sem-pli-ci-tà più m'in-na-mo-ra. A-ma-lo, a-ma-lo, chè n'è de-gno, e se mai per a-mar-lo con più ac-ce-so de-sio ti bi-so-gnas-se un cor pren-di-ti, pren-di-ti il mi-o.

Attacca subito l'aria

71. *Aria*

ed il mio a-mo-re u -ni-sci, se ti bi-so-gna il mio co-re ed il mio a-

mo-re, pren-di-ti u -ni-sci, u -ni-sci col tuo a -mor____, col tuo a -mor.

Cadenza

tutti

Co - sì po - trai

solo

quan-to vor - rai   a - mar sì de - gno spo-so   con l'u-no e l'al - tro, e l'al-tro   cor.

Co - sì po - trai   quan-to vor-rai   a - mar,   a - mar sì de - gno   spo-so   con l'u-no e

l'al-tro   cor,   e l'al - - tro cor.

tutti

Da capo

Costanza e Roberto

72. *Recitativo*

Roberto
Un Prin - ci - pe in - fe - li - ce po - treb - be in sì bel gior - no u - na gra - zia ot - te - ner da u - na Re -

Costanza
gi - na? Pur - ch'ei non chie - da a - mo - ri quan - to chie - de ot - ter - rà, co - sì pro - met - to. Lie - ve è la gra - zia

e mol - to da - gli a - mo - ri lon - ta - na, an - zi di - ver - sa. Ab - bia - la dun - que. Al -

le pro - mes - se ag - giun - gi la re - gia fe'. La re - gia fe' s'im - pe - gni, or, che

bra - mi da me? Du - bi - to an - co - ra che tu poi mi scher - ni - sca e mi de - ri - da. No, no,

va - no e il so - spet - to. Ec - co - ti dun - que il fer - ro, ec - co - ti il pet - to, vo - glio, vo - glio che tu m'uc -

ci - da. O Dio! Non pos - so. L'au - to - ri - tà del - la re - al pro - mes - sa i miei vo - ti as - si - cu - ra.

A che pen - si? A che ba - di? U - na Re - gi - na vi - li - pen - de in tal gui - sa e di - so -

no-ra la da-ta fe'? Non son Re-gi-na an-co-ra. Spo-sa d'un gran Mo-nar-ca

in que-sto gior-no, il tuo fa-to a re-gnar già ti de-sti-na. T'uc-ci-de-rò quan-do sa-

rò Re-gi-na. Già sei, già ti com-prai col prez-zo de' miei pian-ti que-sto dia-

de-ma e que-sto tro-no re-gal che og-gi fa-sto-sa a-scen-di, io cer-co la tua glo-ria

e tu la of-fen-di? Di que-sta glo-ria io non cu-ra-va, in-gra-to, tu che l'ap-prez-zi

tan-to e tan-to l'a-mi se-gui-la a tuo pia-cer, da que-sta glo-ria ot-ter-rai ciò che bra-mi.

A lei por-gi i tuoi prie-ghi, a lei do-na i tuoi vez-zi, dil-le, mio ben, mio Nu-me,

e con gio-ia a-mo-ro-sa ab-brac-cia in que-sta glo-ria or la tua spo-sa.

73. *Aria*

Oc-chi bel-li, oc-chi bel-li, a-stri d'a-mo-re, io vi mo-stro a-per-to il co-re, lo ve-

de-te, lo ve-de-te pien di stra-li e di fa-vil-le, di stra-li pie-no e di fa-vil-le?

Io vi mo-stro a-per-to il co-re, lo ve-de-te, oc-chi bel-li, vi mo-stro il co-re pien di stra - li e di fa-vil-le, pien di

183

Costanza, Gualtiero e guardie

74. *Recitativo*

Gualtiero: Ot-to-ne a me si gui-di. Ap-pun-to, o bel-la, col de-sio ti cer-ca-va.

partono alcune guardie

Costanza: Os-se-qui-o-sa mi pre-sen-to al mio

Gualt.: Re. Fa-ma, cre-do io te-me-ra-ria e bu-giar-da, spar-se che al-le mie noz-ze con mol-ta pe-na il tuo bel ge-nio as-sen-te, che fan-ciul-la in-no-cen-te con de-stra an-cor di lat-te hai pro-mes-sa la fe-de, hai do-na-to l'af-fet-to i vo-ti ed i so-spi-ri a un al-tro og-get-to, che gui-da-ta al mio no-do da ti-ran-ni-ca for-za, a me por-ta-sti un co-re sen-za co-re, un' al-ma sen-za vi-ta e sen-za a-mo-re.

Cost.: Si-gnor, di que-sta fa-ma io nul-la so. Cor-ra-do te-sti-mo-nio ti sia dell'o-ne-stà, dell'in-no-cen-za mi-a. Ol-tre la fe' del Prin-ci-pe vor-rei qual-che pro-va più cer-ta. (A-i-ta, o Dei!)

Gualt.: Dim-mi:

Cost.: (Che mai far deg-gio?)

Gualt.: Se io son da te lon-ta-no, t'af-flig-gi? Ti di-spia-ce?

Cost.: Non ho tut-ta la pa-ce.

Gualt.: E se poi son pre-sen-te, ti ral-le-gri? Ne go-di?

Cost.: Sen-to non so qual gio-ia.

Gualt.: So-la e fra te par-lan-do mi no-mi-ni ta-lo-ra?

Cost.: Spes-so, e con pe-na an-co-ra.

Gualt.: Que-sti son tut-ti, o bel-la, se-gni d'un cor che m'a-ma, van-ne che al-tro il mio a-mor da te non bra-ma.

75. *Aria*

76. *Recitativo*

lu-so e sprez-za-to   u-sò pria le lu-sin-ghe   in-di il ri-go-re.   A-mi dun-que Gri-sel-da?   A-mor tu so-lo che a ra-pir-la m'in-

dus-se.   E non te-me-sti il mio sde-gno re-a-le?   A-man-do, o Si-re, ciò che a-ma-sti u-na vol-ta   e or più non a-mi

in che, in che t'of-fen-do?   Ot-to-ne, de-gli af-fet-ti del Re quei del vas-sal-lo pren-don re-go-la e nor-ma,

ec-co il tuo fal-lo.   I re-a-ti d'a-mo-re Amo-re as-sol-va, tu pu-re a-ma-sti.   Al mer-to di te, de-gli a-vi, al

san-gue spar-so in prò del mio re-gno,   al-la tua fe-de dia-si l'er-ror. Dia-si l'og-get-to an-co-ra.   Gri-sel-da? Ah, non con-vie-ne

che er-ri fra mon-ti e bo-schi   don-na che fu Re-gi-na e tua con-sor-te,   in-nal-za, in-nal-za un tuo ri-fiu-to   e in

lei per-met-ti   che io, spo-so e e-re-de, a-mi i tuoi pri-mi af-fet-ti.   Qua Gri-sel-da si chia-mi.   Ve-di se io son cle-men-te

piuc-chè non chie-di: il giu-ro, Ot-to-ne,   il giu-ro sul mio dia-de-ma,   al-lo-ra che io mi spo-si a Co-stan-za,   av-rai Gri-

sel-da.   O do-no! O gio-ia!   La-scia che al tuo pie-de re-gal..No,   pri-ma at-ten-di che la gra-zie s'a-dem-pia, e   poi la ren-di.

188

77. Aria

Gualtiero, poi Griselda; guardie

78. Recitativo

79. *Aria*

192

ec - co la gio - ia in sen, la gio-ia in sen.

Pro - va da - rò più bel - la del mio co - stan - te____ a-mo - re can -

gian - do il mio do - lo - re in pla - - - ci - do se - ren, can - gian -

- do il mio do - lo - re in pla - - - - ci - do se - ren.

Da capo

193

80. *Recitativo*

Gualtiero

Pe - no   ma per te pe - no, spo - sa fe - de - le   a - ma - ta spo - sa,   e men - tre

Continuo

6   (6)   #   6

5

mi co-strin-ge em-pio fa - to   ad es-ser te - co un in-giu-sto,   un ti - ran - no,   nel tuo co - re e nel

6   6   ♭7
#4   5

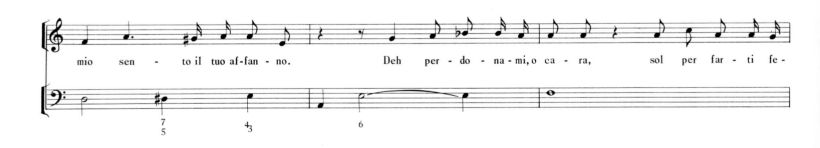

mio sen - to il tuo af-fan - no.   Deh per - do - na - mi, o ca - ra,   sol per far - ti fe -

7   4 3   6
5

10

li - ce   in-fe-li - ce ti ren - do,   sol per-chè t'a - mo a - ni-ma mia   t'of - fen - do.

6   6   ♭6   4 3
#4   6   ♭

Siegue l'Aria

194

81. *Aria*

195

se - no due fiam-mel-le del pa - ri il -lu-stri e bel - le, u - na è la tua bel-lez - za e

l'al - - tra è il tuo va - lor. Bel-lez-za, va-lor, bel-lez - - -

za, bel - lez - za, va - lor.

L'af - fet - to del mio pet - to in am - be si è di - vi - so: a -

do-ro il tuo bel vi-so, a-do-ro il tuo bel cor. In am-be si e di-vi-so: a-do-ro il tuo bel vi-so, il tuo bel

vi-so, a-do-ro, a-do-ro il tuo bel cor, il tuo bel cor. Ho in

tutti

Dal segno

198

Passeggio delizioso nei giardini reali.
Roberto, poi Corrado

82. *Aria*

Co-me va l'a-pe di fio-re in fio - re   fa-sto-so al - te - ro   su-per-bo a-

mo-re   di bel-la in bel-la____ vo-lan-do va_____, di bel-la in bel-la vo-

lan-do   va, vo-lan-do   va,   di fio-re in fio-re   co-me va

200

l'a-pe su-per-bo a-mo - re fa - sto-so al-te - ro di bel-la in bel - la, di bel-la in bel - la vo - lan - - do, vo -

lan - do va, vo - lan - - - - - - do, vo - lan - do va, vo - lan - do

va, vo - lan - do va.

Fe-ri-sce que - sta, ri - sa - na

quel - la, in u-na ac-cen-de la sua fa - cel - la nell' al-tra de-sta la cru-del - tà, la cru-del - tà.

In u-na ac - cen-de   la sua fa - cel-la   nel-l'al-tra de-sta la   cru-del - tà_____ ,

Cadenza

de - sta, de-sta la   cru-del - tà.

tutti

7   7

Dal segno

203

83. Recitativo

Mentre Roberto vuol partire, sopravviene Costanza.

84. *Aria*

205

85. *Recitativo*

giac-chè rea mi la-sci sap-pi tut-to il mio er-ro-re: d'al-tri fia que-sta man, tuo, tuo que-sto co-re.

Rob.
Ah, non dir più che m'a-mi se vuoi che da te lun-ge io por-ti il pie-de, gran lu-sin-ga al-l'in-du-gio è la tua fe-de.

Cost.   Rob.
Più no'l di-rò, mia vi-ta. Van-ne sì, van-ne pur t'af-fret-to anch' io, gran ci-men-to è l'in-du-gio al-l'o-nor mio. Co-

Cost.   Rob.   Cost.
stan-za... Mi ab-ban-do-ni? Co-sì la mia for-tu-na co-sì, co-sì co-man-da il tuo de-sti-no. O

Violino I

Violino II

Viola

Rob.   Cost.   Rob.
Di-o! Ri-cor-da-ti di me, pen-sa.. Ro-ber-to, non più, che tu m'uc-ci-di. E tu l'al-ma dal-l'al-ma or mi di-vi-di.

86. *Duetto*

*Figures in brackets have been added in a different hand in the London manuscript.

Segue subito
Scena x

Re - ste - rò, ma ser - ban - do-ti il mio a-mo-

Par - ti - rò, ma la - scian - do-ti il mio co - re

re a di - spet-to di quel Fa - to che spie - ta - to la mia fe - de mi ra -

a di - spet-to di quel Fa - to che spie - ta - to la tua fe - de mi ra -

pì, che spie - ta - to la mia fe - de ti ra - pì.

pì, che spie - ta - to la tua fe - de mi ra - pì.

Dal segno

212

87. *Recitativo*

Griselda (a Costanza): Con sì pu-di-co af-fet-to voi con-sor-te al-lo spo-so? (a Roberto) Con si o-ne-sto ri-spet-to vie-ni a-mi-co al-la reg-gia? È que-sta, è que-sta dell'I-me-neo la fe-de? Dell'o-spi-zio la leg-ge? Nel dì del-le sue noz-ze, nel suo stes-so sog-gior-no, un ma-ri-to non a-mi? Un Re non te-mi? O in-giu-ste fiam-me, o vi-li-pen-di e-stre-mi! (Mi-se-ra!) (Qual con-si-glio!) An-cor, an-cor ta-ce-te?

88. *Recitativo*

Gualtiero: Gri-sel-da. Costanza: (Ahi-mè!) Roberto: (Son mor-to.) Gualt.: Per-chè tu d'i-ra ac-ce-sa? E voi bell'al-me, per-chè con-fu-se? E do-vrò Griselda: dir-lo? Gualt.: E-spo-ni: che u-di-sti? Che ve-de-sti? Gris.: Nul-la fuor-chè il mio fa-to sem-pre ver me cru-del sem-pre, sem-pre spie-ta-to. Gualt.: Il Prin-ci-pe Cor-ra-do ciò che av-ven-ne mi nar-ri, tu se par-li o se ta-ci o-gnor m'of-fen-di. Corrado: Il tut-to, o Si-re, in po-che no-te in-ten-di. Rob.: (Non v'è più scam-po.) Cost.: (Ahi sor-te!) Corr.: Vi-cen-de-vo-le af-fet-to di Ro-ber-to e Co-

stan-za u-ni-sce i co-ri, u-dì Gri-sel-da i lo-ro ac-cen-ti e vi-de le lor de-stre im-pal-ma-te.

20
Gualt.
E per-ciò tan-to sde-gno? Ben si ve-de che na-ta sei, Gri-sel-da, tra bo-schi. At-ten-do io for-se che tu le par-ti a-

25
dem-pia d'e-splo-ra-tri-ce o di mi-ni-stra e ser-va? Cor-reg-gi, cor-reg-gi il fa-sto e i tuoi do-ve-ri os-ser-va.

Gris. Gualt. Gris. Gualt. **30** Gris.
Quel ze-lo... Io non t'el chie-do. Il ri-spet-to... Lo de-vi al-la re-gia con-sor-te. Il tuo o-

Gualt.
nor, la tua glo-ri-a? A te, a te che im-por-ta che la bel-la Co-stan-za ab-bia più d'un a-man-te che di-

35 Cost.) a 2 Gualt.
Rob.)
vi-da il suo cor? Che a-mi a sua vo-glia o Ro-ber-to o Gual-tier? (Nu-mi che a-scol-to!) Ti sov-ven-ga il suo

Gris. Gualt. Gris. Gualt. **40**
gra-do. E di Re-gi-na. Il tuo uf-fi-zio? E d'an-cel-la. E se ta-lor per al-tri ar-der la

Gris. Gualt. Gris. Gualt.
mi-ri? Cie-che a-vrò le pu-pil-le. Se so-spi-rar la sen-ti? Sor-do l'u-di-to. E se a-mo-ro-sa pren-de di Ro-ber-to la

45
ma-no non ti tur-bar, non t'a-di-rar, ma pen-sa che Ro-ber-to e Co-stan-za fin dal-l'e-tà bam-bi-na s'a-ma-va-no a vi-

214

cen-da, ed a vi-cen-da s'an-no-da-van le de-stre e co-me al-lo-ra gli af-fet-ti lor so-no in-no-cen-ti an-co-ra.

Gris. L'al-te tue leg-gi e se-gui-rò qual deb-bo, e sof-fren-do e ta-cen-do. (Bar-ba-ro mio de-sti-no io non t'in-ten-do.)

Corr. Io, Si-gnor, t'as-si-cu-ro co-sì del-la tua spo-sa co-me del mio ger-ma-no in-no-

cen-te e il de-sio, pu-di-co il co-re, nè of-fen-de la tua glo-ria il lo-ro a-mo-re. (parte) Cost. (Tre-mo.) Rob. (Pa-ven-to.) Gualt. Or non e-stin-gua in voi

fred-da te-ma im-por-tu-na i ca-sti ar-do-ri, cer-ti te-ne-ri af-fet-ti che del tem-po e del cor fi-gli pur so-no per-do-no al

ge-nio ed al-l'e-tà per-do-no. Cost. Per-do-no io non vor-rei se of-fe-sia-ve-sti l'o-nor tuo, l'o-nor

mio, con om-bra di pen-sie-ro o di con-si-glio. Rob. Un vo-lon-ta-rio e-si-lio quin-di io pren-dea...Ta-ce-te, Gualt.

che più del vo-stro a-mo-re la di-scol-pa mi spia-ce. Con fug-gir da Co-stan-za reo di-ven-ti, o Ro-ber-to, e tu più

rea se da lui ti di-vi-di: pro-se-gui-te, pro-se-gui-te ad a-mar-vi e sia-te, e sia-te fi-di.

89. Quartetto

216

(Ma pu - re è mio de - lit - to, de

mio spa - ven - to l'i - stes - sa fe - del - tà, ma pu - re è mio spa - ven -

mio spa - ven - to l'i - stes - sa fe - del - tà, è mio spa - ven - to,

ma pu - re è mio tor - men -

lit - to l'i - stes - sa, de - lit - to,

- to l'i - stes - sa, l'i - stes - sa fe - del - tà___, spa - ven - to,

spa - ven - to l'i - stes - sa, spa - ven - to l'i - stes - sa fe - del -

- to l'i - stes - sa, tor - men - to,

de - lit - to,   ep - pu - re è mio de - lit   -   to, è mio de - lit - to   l'i - stes - sa

spa - ven - to   l'i - stes - sa

tà _____, spa - ven - to   l'i - stes - sa

tor - men - to,   l'i - stes - sa   fe - del - tà,   l'i - stes - sa
tutti   solo   tutti

fe - del - tà.)

fe - del - tà.)

fe - del - tà.)

fe - del - tà.)   Fin -

Costanza

90. *Recitativo*

Costanza

Nu – mi! Sa-ria mai ve – ro ciò che un so-a – ve e lu-sin-ghie-ro af – fet – to mi sus-sur – ra nel pet – to?

Continuo

Io più non sen-to quel-l'in-ter – no tor-men-to che pur dian-zi sen-ti – a. Pen-so a Gual-tie – ro, pen-so a Cor-ra-do . . .

Ba-sta, non in-ten-do me stes-sa ma in sì dol-ce sem-bian-za in-gan-nar-mi non può la mia spe-ran-za.

91. *Aria*

Allegrissimo

Oboe I

Violino I, II

Costanza

Continuo

Se va-ga se bel-la se fi – da son' io, bell' i – do-lo

Che io

la - sci d'a-mar-ti? Che io pen-si a la-sciar-ti? Mi sen - to lan-gui-re, mi sen - to mo-ri-re, pos-

si - bil, pos-si - bil non è. D'a-mar - ti che io la-sci, che io pen-si a la-sciar-ti? Mi sen - to lan-

gui-re, mi sen - to mo-ri - - re, pos-si - bil non è, no, no, no, no, pos-si - bil non è.

Da capo

Scena xiii

Anfiteatrale che si va preparando con il-
luminazioni e altre pompe per le nozze.
Griselda.

92. *Recitativo*

Terminate, o ministri, l'alta pompa solenne, il dì già stanco ravvivate coi lumi e più giulivo del suo Signor senta la reggia i voti. Legge è del mio Gualtier che io stessa affretti e renda più superba delle tragedie mie la scena acerba.

Scena Ultima

Gualtiero, Roberto, Ottone, Costanza, Griselda e Corrado con Everardo.
Cavalieri, donzelle, guardie e popoli spettatori.

93. *Recitativo*

Griselda. Altro non manca che il tuo sovrano impero. Mi è di pena infinita ogni momento che a Costanza m'invola. Anche Griselda amasti. La tua viltà le chiare fiamme estinse. Per l'illustre tua sposa ardano eterne. Ah! non voler da lei della mia tolleranza i rari esempi, mal può darli Costanza, gentil di sangue e poco, qual io vil donna, alle sciagure avvezza. (O bontade!) (O vir-

225

226

Ma che ad Ot - ton mi spo - si, che sia d'al - tri il mio co - re, la mia fe - de, il mio a-mo - re? Ah __

__ Gual - tier, mi per-do - na, è que - sto, è que-sto il ca - ro ben che so - lo li - be - ro dal tuo im-

Gualt.

pe - ro io m'ho ser-ba-to: tua vis-si e tua mor - rò, spo-so a-do-ra-to. (La-gri-me non u - sci - te.) A che, a che più

Gris.

tar-di? E - leg-gi: Ot - to - ne o mor - te. Mor - te, mor-te, o Si-gnor! Ser - vi, cu - sto - di, cer -

ca-te ne' tor-men-ti, a-guz-za-te ne' fer-ri, ne' ve-le-ni i-na-spri-te la mor-te mia; chi vuol tra voi la glo-ria del pri - mo

Violino I

Violino II

Viola

(s'inginocchia)

col-po? Ah, spo-so! al - la tua ma-no il chie-do e pro-stra-ta te'l chie-do. Fa che io va-da a-gli E-li - si om-bra su-per-ba

228

d'u-na mor-te sì ca-ra   i-vi ad-di-tan-do le mie bel-le fe - ri - te, o-pra già de' tuoi lu-mi,   or del tuo brac-cio.   (Non più,

non più, mio cor, non più.)   Spo-sa,   spo-sa t'ab-brac-cio.   (Mi - se-ro Ot-ton!)

Gualt.

(a Gris. sollevandola)   Ott.

Corno I

Corno II

Violino I
Oboe I

Violino II
Oboe II

Viola

Coro

Soprano

Vi - va,   vi-va Gri-sel - da,   vi-va Gri-sel - da,   vi - va,   vi - va,   vi - va.

Alto

Vi - va,   vi-va Gri-sel - da,   vi - va Gri-sel - da,   vi - va,   vi - va,   vi - va.

Tenore

Vi - va,   vi-va Gri-sel - da,   vi-va Gri-sel - da,   vi - va,   vi - va,   vi - va.

Continuo

94. Ensemble

Il Fine

L.D.M.V.

APPENDIX

At a late stage in the composition of *Griselda* Scarlatti cancelled portions of his original score, replacing some of them by different versions. The Appendix includes all the rejected items that are now recoverable from the autograph manuscript of Acts I and III in the British Museum. Included also is one aria from the Berlin manuscript ("Credi Amor") which does not appear in any other source. Details of the location of all these items in relation to the final version of the opera will be found in the Critical Notes; see also Introduction, footnote 3.

Editorial practice follows that in the main body of the edition except that the following details have been kept exactly as they appear in *A:* spelling, punctuation, and capitalization of the text; designation of instruments; bass figures; time signatures; notation of triplets. All cautionary accidentals have been retained, in modernized form. The sign ‿‖ signifies a tie necessitated by a measure being divided at the end of a line in *A*.

Folio numbers refer to *A*. Parentheses around folio numbers indicate a passage beginning elsewhere than at the beginning of a page.

PASSAGES IN THE APPENDIX

Sinfonia per lo sbarco

Aria

Earlier version of Number 21

Oubuoè solo / **Unis.** / **Cost.**

Go - di, bell' Al - ma, go - di, bell' al - ma, go - di, ral -

le - gra-ti, con - so - la-ti, già che la mia gran-dez - za è tua fe - li - ci - tà___, fe - li - ci - tà,

go - di, go - di, go - di, bell' al - ma, go - di, ral - le - gra-ti, con -

so - la - ti, gia che la mia gran-dez - za è tua fe - li - ci - tà. Bell' al - ma, ral - le - gra-ti, bell' al - ma con-

In A the oboe part is written below the violins.

so-la-ti, go-di, go-di, già che la mia gran-dez-za è tua fe-li-ci-tà _____, è tua,

è tua fe-li-ci-tà.

Re-gi-na mi vo-le-sti, Re-

gi-na mi fa-ce-sti, il Cie-lo del tuo ze-lo mer-cè ti ren-de-rà. Re-gi-na mi vo-le-sti, Re-

solo

tutti

gi-na mi fa-ce-sti, il Cie-lo del tuo ze-lo mer-cè _____ mer-cè ti ren-de-rà

Da capo

solo

tutti

1) *apparently first begun:*   2) *apparently begun:*

Aria

Originally at the end of Number 32

Aria

Originally in III, xi, after measure 56 of Number 88

cer. Sa-prò con al-ma for - te, e fin - ge-re, e fin - ge-re, e ta-cer, e ta-cer, e e ta-cer.

Di - rò, ch'er-rai, di - rò, ch'er-rai col guar - do, che il la-bro fù bu-giar - do, e

solo

sol de la mia sor - te _____ mi pren-de-rò pen - sier. Di - rò ch'er-rai col guar - do, che il la-bro fù bu-

tutti

giar-do, e sol de la mia sor - te mi pren-de-rò pen - sier, sol _____ mi pren-de-rò pen - sier.

solo

da Capo

tutti

Recitative and Aria

Originally separate scene in the place of Number 89

fol. 114ᵛ

Sei trop-po bel-la, sei trop-po A-man - te, trop-po fe-de-le, trop-po co-stan - te; la tua bel-

lez-za mi le-ga, mi le-ga___ il co - re, ed il tuo A-mo-re mi le - - - -

-ga il piè, ed il tuo A-mo-re mi le-ga, mi le - - - - - ga il piè.

fol. 116

da Capo

da Capo

solo   tutti

Aria

Perhaps originally at the beginning of III, xiii

1) *sic*. Probably ♫ ♪ ♪ | ♪ ♫ ♫ | (*cf.* mm. 70–71)
vi - so ch'ar-de di

da Capo

Recitative
Earlier version of Number 14

Recitative
Earlier version of Number 18

(fol. 36*)

250

Fragments and short revisions

From Number 5

From Number 7

1) *Many notes uncertain in these two measures.*

From Number 11

From Number 13

From Number 17

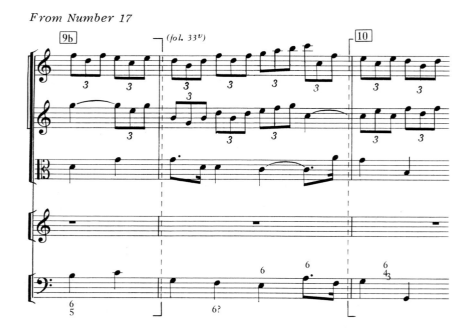

From Number 19

From Number 27

255

From Number 31

From Number 36

From Number 69

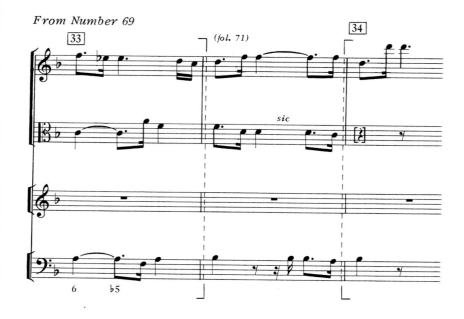

From Number 81

(Fl.)

(Oub.)

From Number 82

From Number 84

258

From Number 86

From Number 13

cru - de - il mio Fa - to mi vol - le gui - dar___ mi vol - le gui - dar -le il

From Number 15

[notes partially erased]

-tà   Chi   sa? chi sa   se be - ne il fa - to si mo - stra   tan - ta

[crossed out -]

From Number 34

Voi,   voi so - spi - ra - te,   voi so - spi - ra - te bel - lez - ze a - ma - te bel - lez   - ze a - ma   -   te

or(?)

- ze a-ma - te

1) *These four notes partially erased*

2) *These six words crossed out*

3) *Erasure, unclear*

From Number 81

1) *half-rest in MS*

From Number 91

te, per te, per te per te son bel-la, bel-la, va-ga, va-ga, fi-da fi-da per te— per— te, per te, per te, per te.

From Number 8

il cor ne serbo: e puoi sof-frir ch'al-tra s'u-sur-pi un fre-gio al tuo mer-to do-vu-to? fre-gi piu che Re-a-li a no-bil

Al-ma so-no in-no-cen-za, e fe-de. ser-bo

1) *From here, erased but faintly legible under notes of m12b*

From Number 16

-tu-na. e qual im-pe-ro a-gua-glia, se fai giu-di-ce A-mo-re, la glo-ria d'im-pe-rar nel tuo bel co-re? e pur

-rai di Ro-ber-to an-co-ra il no-me. per-do-no, per-do-no al tuo do-lo-re que-sti te-ne-ri ol-trag-gi. il Cie-lo, i Nu-mi

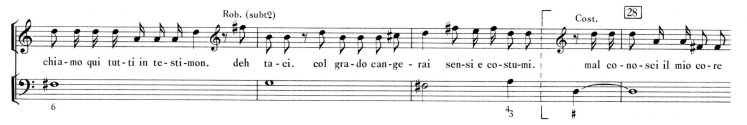

chia-mo qui tut-ti in te-sti-mon. deh ta-ci. col gra-do can-ge-rai sen-si e co-stu-mi. mal co-no-sci il mio co-re

1) *Possible original state of this measure*

2) *These eleven notes have been altered; original illegible*

From Number 18

From Number 22

1) *Some indistinct erasures here*

2) *Possible earlier version of measures 15–16 (indistinct)*

From Number 25

From Number 26

1) First half of this measure is a reconstruction.

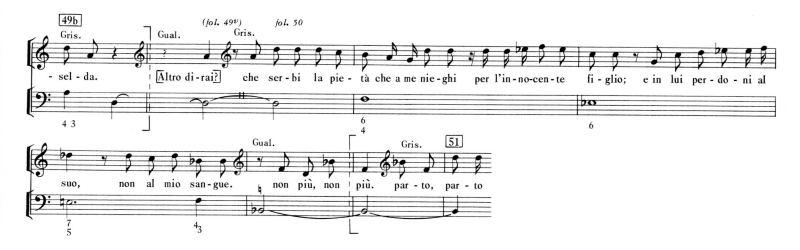

From Number 28

From Number 35

From Number 74

From Number 85

From Number 87

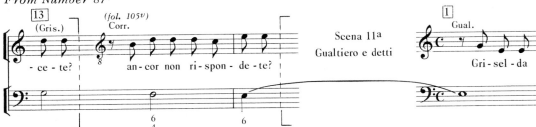

From Number 88

Aria "Credi Amor"

(II, ix) in B, pp. 166—169

se del Nu - me è pro - prio il Be - ne: per - che spar-gi af - fan - ni, e pe - ne,

solo

ò per-che trà gl'al - tri De - i re-gna un Nu-me tra - di - tor? per - che per-che? per-che spar-gi af - fan - ni, e

[40]

[45]

pe - ne, ò per-che trà gl'al - tri De - i re-gna un Nu-me tra - di - tor? tra - di - tor?

[Da capo]

[Da capo]

tutti

Translations

Aria "Godi, bell'alma" (earlier version of Number 21)

   Translation in Libretto

Aria "Non lasciar d'amar" (originally at the end of Number 32)

   Do not cease to love him who loves you, as long as your soul is free. When you are at last a spouse, you will shyly and modestly obey honor more than love, duty more than beauty. Do not, etc.

Aria "Se amori ascoltero" (originally in Act III, after measure 56 of Number 88)

   If I hear lovemaking, if I see embraces, I shall know how to pretend, with a strong mind, and be silent. I shall say that my look was mistaken, that my lips were lying, and I shall think only of my fate. If I hear, etc.

Recitativo "Intesi, o m'ingannai" and Aria "Non so che sia" (originally separate scene in place of Number 89)

   ROB. Have I heard aright, or was I deceived?
   COST. Was I awake or dreaming?
   ROB. Gualtiero wants me not to leave?
   COST. My bridegroom wants me to love you?
   ROB. Ah, Costanza . . .
   COST. Ah, Roberto . . .
   ROB. . . . often poison is mixed with a sweet drink . . .
   COST. . . . often a fair clear sky conceals a storm . . .
   ROB. I know that staying is a risk.
   COST. I know that it is a sin to love you.
   ROB. What are you thinking?
   COST. What is your decision?
   ROB. To obey, with fear.
   COST. To love you, with trembling.
   ROB. I do not know what will happen, my soul; I cannot leave you. You are too beautiful, too loving, too faithful, too steadfast; your beauty holds my heart in thrall, and love for you my feet. I do not know, etc.

Aria "Pargoletto che porti felice" (perhaps originally at the beginning of III, xiii)

   CORR. Little one, you who bring joy to the beautiful countenance of your mother and to the great heart of your father: I see the glories of your forbears rising again in your lovely face, the face that glows with joy and love. Little one, etc.

Recitativo "Germani, e ben entrambi" (earlier version of Number 14)

   Translation in Libretto

Recitativo "L'arcano in te racchiudi" (earlier version of Number 18)

   GUAL. Keep the secret to yourself.
   CORR. My straightforward faithfulness is quite well known to you.
   GUAL. My beloved Roberto . . . But where is Costanza?
   ROB. She just now went toward that fountain.
   GUAL. Ottone, tell her that I am longing for her.
   OTT. She is already returning.
   CORR. Look at her, and say whether a fairer ideal ever came down to the earth from the sphere of Love?

GUAL. Fair Costanza, how glad I am to meet you: and what tenderness and happiness, children of love, I feel on embracing you!

COST. My Lord: my soul, taken aback (*etc. as in Number 18*)

Cancelled passages from Recitativo, Number 32

CORR. Pity is the daughter of a noble soul.

COST. And the king, whom she loved so much, how can he be so cruel and heartless towards her? Ah, I fear Griselda's example for myself.

CORR. A vain fear. She was born a humble shepherdess, in a rustic dwelling.

COST. I too am of unknown parentage.

CORR. I assure you that you are the daughter of a king; and your regal nature gives proof of your origins.

COST. It is my misfortune that I do not know them yet.

CORR. It is your good luck to see that a king adores you. But with what kind of love do you requite Gualtiero's?

COST. With that which is suitable for a bride.

CORR. And that for a lover, for whom do you keep it? That is the most tender affection. The spouse loves the one she ought, the lover the one she chooses. The genius of the latter is love, of the former, duty.

COST. Alas!

CORR. Do not blush; more than Gualtiero, you love Roberto.

Cancelled passage from Recitativo, Number 72

ROB. Blind severity regards duty as an error, love as a fault.

COST. What duty compels you to will your own distress and to make you a tyrant to me no less than to yourself?

ROB. But who could . . .

COST. No more; I disdain to hear you.

ROB. You are forbidding a dying man to utter his last words?

COST. And for whom are you dying?

ROB. O Heaven! Only to you is it not known that you are the cause of my dying?

COST. You are dying for me? Shall I believe it? Is it really true? Can I trust you? Ah, liar!

Aria "Credi Amor" (Act II, Scene ix) in *B*, pp. 166–169

Believe me, o Love, you are unworthy of the fair name of Love. If good is the characteristic of a god, why do you scatter trouble and sorrow? O, why, among the other gods, does a treacherous god rule?

269

LIBRETTO

Argument

Gualtiero, King of Sicily (given this rank in the drama for the decorum and nobility of the stage, although according to history he was only Marquis of Saluzzo), having fallen in love with a shepherdess named Griselda, whom he had often seen while hunting, took her to wife, since this was the only way he could conquer her virtue and satisfy the passion of his love.

A marriage of such unequal rank served the people as a motive for murmuring against their prince; and after the birth of a girl, the first fruit of this marriage, they would have gone on to some kind of rebellion had Gualtiero not immediately stifled it by giving out that he had had the daughter (here called Costanza) killed. In fact, he sent her secretly to another prince, a friend of his (who is here called Corrado, Prince of Apulia) for him to bring her up in secret.

Costanza had already reached the age of fifteen years, without her or anyone else (except Gualtiero and Corrado) knowing who her parents were, when the people, on account of another child born later to Griselda, rebelled again. They were egged on chiefly by Ottone, a noble knight of the realm and a secret admirer of the Queen; wherefore Gualtiero decided to stop their disorders by the fiction of repudiating his consort and marrying another lady of higher birth. He resorted to this device because, knowing full well Griselda's virtue, he wished to furnish public proof of it, so that his subjects would likewise recognize it and be persuaded that she was not debasing the rank of queen by the lowliness of her birth, but was ennobling it through the greatness of her soul.

For this purpose he wrote and ordered Corrado to bring him his daughter, in appearance to be his bride. Thereupon he told Griselda of her rejection and sent her back to her forest, which she suffered with a strength and courage which were more than manly, with the admiration of the people and of her husband himself.

Together with Costanza, Roberto, younger brother of Corrado, was brought to the place. Having grown up and been educated together with the princess, he loved her tenderly; and this love was not only reciprocated by Costanza, but was also approved by Corrado, who intended for them to marry.

Intermingled with the true passions of Roberto and Costanza, the pretended severity of Gualtiero and the true persecutions of Ottone (who, in the misfortunes of Griselda, has hopes of gaining her) form the plot of the drama, with the happenings that take place in its course. Many of these are not inventions of the poet, although they may seem to be such, but historical events.

That visit of Costanza to Griselda's hut, taken there on purpose by her father under the pretext of a hunt, is historical fact. Likewise, that heightening of the pulse and that beating of the heart which the mother and daughter both feel on seeing each other for the first time, unbeknownst to each other, are true to history. Costanza's request to Gualtiero to have Griselda as her servant is historically accurate. Historically true, finally, is the great constancy shown by Griselda in the face of the many indignities heaped on her by her husband, until he, softened and overcome by her expressions of affection, embraced her weeping, telling her of Costanza's true status and the purpose of his pretended hostility.

The vicissitudes of Griselda are related by Francesco Petrarca in his minor works in Latin, by Filippo Foresti of Bergamo in his Supplement to the Chronicles, and by other famous authors.

Cast of Characters

King Gualtiero of Sicily
Queen Griselda, his wife
Princess Costanza, their daughter
Ottone, Grandee of the realm
Prince Corrado of Apulia
Roberto, younger brother of Corrado
Everardo, another child of Griselda and Gualtiero

In this translation the number of scenes and the references to their musical settings have been adapted to conform to the present edited score, which represents Scarlatti's final version of *Griselda*. For details see the Appendix and the Critical Notes. Lines bracketed in the outside margin do not appear in the score.

ACT I

Scene i
Magnificent room, destined for public audiences. On one side, lofty dais with two thrones. On the other, Grandees of the Realm and people. Military orders in the background. Gualtiero with his royal retinue, who take their places around his throne.

2   GUAL. This, o people, is the day on which your King takes his laws from you. To you, a woman taken from the forest, a woman accustomed to tend herds and flocks, does not seem worthy of my couch and throne. As such, I loved Griselda; but as such, you have scorned her. Now finally I behold her with your eyes; I am sending her, rejected, back to her forest; and I am replacing my love with your love. *(Mounts the throne.)*

3   PEOPLE. Now you are great, and now you are a King, now that you add to your glory the victory which love gave you over love. Now you are great, etc.

Scene ii
GRISELDA, *with her retinue, and the above*

4   GRIS. Behold, sire, your humble servant.

GUAL. Come, o Queen; for weighty matters I desire your presence.

GRIS. You know that this soul hangs entirely on your lips.

GUAL. Sit down.

GRIS. I obey. *(Sits beside* GUALTIERO.*)*

GUAL. Be so kind as to remember the course of past events. Tell me who I was, and who you were.

GRIS. (A lofty beginning!) I was born in a lowly hovel, and you in a royal palace.

GUAL. Your occupation was . . . ?

GRIS. To tend the flocks.

GUAL. And mine . . . ?

GRIS. To make laws for the world.

GUAL. How did you come to the throne?

GRIS. It was your kindness, which deigned to raise me from the nothingness of my lowly, abject poverty.

GUAL. As such, I made you Queen?

GRIS. And I was your servant.

GUAL. And as such, I took you to my bosom?

GRIS. And I took you to my heart.

GUAL. (Such faith and such love could deserve no less than a kingdom.) Did we have children?

GRIS. One daughter.

GUAL. And she was then taken from you when she was still in the cradle?

GRIS. Nor did I ever have any word of her thereafter.

GUAL. How long ago?

GRIS. The year has retraced its steps fifteen times.

GUAL. Did you feel sorrow at this?

GRIS. A sign from you was law to my grief.

GUAL. Know, then, that I was an executioner, not a father to her.

GRIS. It was your blood, and you had the right to shed it as you desired.

GUAL. And you love me, even though I was cruel?

GRIS. I would not love you any less, o Heavens, if you were even to shed my own.

GUAL. And finally?

GRIS. From our chaste embraces there was born another noble offspring, Everardo, your only delight.

GUAL. In so long a time, was I displeasing to you? Did I harm you?

GRIS. I had only gracious treatment from you.

GUAL. Of what I have done, I do not repent; may Heaven be my witness. But yet, I must take back my gifts. Sometimes the king must obey his subjects, and be a tyrant over himself to preserve his rule.

GRIS. Where you reign, I condemn all other reasons.

GUAL. Sicily, over which I rule, refuses to obey me. She accuses me of having debased the royal couch by mating with you, and will not accept its Queen from the forest, where you were born. Therefore she has forced me to provide a bride of royal blood for the royal couch.

GRIS. The subject province, which suffered me for fifteen years as its Queen, only now rejects me?

GUAL. It has been chafing against the yoke for a long time. I already shed the blood of my daughter for reasons of state. This cruel sacrifice diminished hatred somewhat, but did not extinguish it. Now that it sees an heir arising in my son, the realm is again angry and insults me.

GRIS. Ah, if Everardo severs such fine bonds of love, let Everardo too . . . No, no; let Griselda die; for if I am a wife, I am a mother too.

GUAL. You are no longer my wife. *(Comes down from the throne.)*

GRIS. Pardon me, o my King, if I have been too bold, and if I have perhaps been too slow in giving back to you a name so dear to me. Your wish should have been law to my feelings. Behold, I divest myself of crown and scepter; and to that right hand which placed them on me and gave them to me, I return them. *(Gives crown and scepter to* GUALTIERO, *who takes them and has them placed on the throne.)*

GUAL. (Be firm, o my soul!)

GRIS. If in this way I please you, I find gain even in my loss.

In wishing what you desire, in desiring what pleases   5
you, I shall always, o belovèd, find my joy and my peace. Do not demand that I not love you, do not forbid me to adore you; tell me, "Griselda, die!" and I shall gladly die. In wishing, etc. *(On the way out, she meets* OTTONE, *who stops her.)*

Scene iii
OTTONE *and the aforementioned*

OTT. *(To* GRISELDA*)* Stay, and you shall find out.   6

GRIS. What can it be? *(Turns back.)*

GUAL. What news do you bring, Ottone?

OTT. Prince Corrado is already landing at the nearby port on a lordly ship, and is bringing to you, as he was commanded, the royal bride.

GUAL. The royal bride? Farewell, Griselda; I go.

GRIS. Where?

GUAL. To meet her.

GRIS. In such haste? and so joyfully? O Heaven! Was the blow which was to kill me so near? So, you are leaving me? So, I lose you?

GUAL. (*To* OTTONE) Let us go; I am awaited.

GRIS. Do you not even grant one last embrace, one last look, to me and my misfortune, before giving yourself to someone else?

GUAL. You are asking too much of me.

GRIS. So, Gualtiero, farewell. (O husband! O kingdom! O bitter and wicked fate!)

7   GUAL. The love of a ruler does not sigh for two eyes which seem like stars, for two eyes which dart arrows. The eyes which make him a lover are bright and beautiful enough when they are royal eyes. The love of a ruler does not sigh, etc.

Scene iv
GRISELDA *and others*

8   OTT. Queen; if you heed any more, you are no longer Queen.

GRIS. How much this man has always importuned me!

OTT. From your brow the crown is already falling. The only one able to keep it for you is Ottone, a faithful subject and a loving admirer.

GRIS. He who is taking my crown from me is taking from me a gift which he gave; and though I abandon the outwards signs of a queen, I keep a queen's heart.

OTT. And can you suffer another woman to take from you a sign of honor which is due to your merit?

GRIS. Signs of honor which are more than royal, for a noble heart, are innocence and faith.

OTT. I, if you command it, will restrain the daring of this over-bold crowd. I will attack the palace; I will upset Gualtiero's approaching nuptials; I will kill him who takes from you the title of queen and that of wife.

GRIS. Evil man, would you dare do this? And do you ask me, you overweening fellow, for my assent? Do you believe that I am this kind of person?

OTT. Think how much an unjust rejection is costing you; and how much you are losing by refusing the assistance of my sword.

GRIS. After all, what am I losing?

OTT. Your kingdom.

GRIS. It was not mine.

OTT. Your husband.

GRIS. I carry him in my heart.

OTT. Your son.

GRIS. He is his father's.

OTT. A loving glance, a sweet hope, just give me, o my idol, I swear to you . . .

GRIS. I care nothing for your favor; I despise your longings; I hate your love. At the price of guilt, I have no desire for rule. I shall gladly go where Heaven decrees for me; as long as my senses are under my control, I am queen.

In my bitter sorrow, let your heart not deceive you with vain hopes. You will see that I am stronger than my cruel fate; you will see that love has given me faith and steadfastness as a spirit. In my bitter sorrow, etc.   9

Scene v
OTTONE

OTT. Griselda is too much accustomed to royal garb and pomp not to be cruel to me. She has not yet laid aside her habits of command; and her crown still allows my sighs no success. But, once far from the palace, she will perhaps have pity on my grief. She who as a queen despises me, as a shepherdess will love me. She will abandon her haughtiness and rigor with her greatness; for beauty is more tender-hearted in the wilderness. She who as a queen, etc.   10   11

Scene vi
Seaport near the city. Ships sailing in the distance. A richly decorated boat approaches, from which there disembark first ROBERTO, *then* CORRADO *and* COSTANZA, *with a retinue of knights, damsels, and guards.*   12

ROB. How quickly my fate has insisted on steering me to this hated port, when an angry tempest should have driven my weary sails elsewhere. How quickly, etc.   13

CORR. Brother and sister—and both of you I shall call brother and sister, one by affection and one by blood, equally dear—wait for me here a short time, so that I may precede your steps, to announce your arrival to the royal bridegroom.   14

ROB. Ah, be not so quick to hasten my dying.

COST. Ah, let misfortune descend more slowly upon me.

CORR. Be silent, henceforth, before the commands of Heaven; and take on you now the heart, you of a prince, and you of a queen.

ROB. Costanza?

COST. My soul?

ROB. Now what will you do?

COST. I do not know.

CORR. In a few moments I shall return with Gualtiero.

ROB. O suffering!

COST. O weeping!

CORR. (*To* COSTANZA) Do not conceal your stars; do not be bathed in tears, o beautiful eyes, for perhaps love will aid you. Who knows? Who knows? Even if fate shows anger, I cannot believe that it wishes to offend such great beauty with its harshness. Do not, etc.   15

Scene vii
ROBERTO, COSTANZA, *and their retinue*

ROB. Here is the port, here is the shore which is so fatal to me, so happy for you. This land on which you tread, fair lady, is Sicily; and that is the lofty palace, where Gualtiero is awaiting laws from your eyes to give them to his realms.   16

COST. Ah, Roberto, Roberto!

276

ROB. Are you sighing, and accepting your greatness in sorrow?

COST. How much happier would I be to live privately, and far from that palace, in which all greatness will forever be bitter for me, provided that I belong to you and you to me.

ROB. (O belovèd!)

COST. One single glance from you is worth more than all the fortune of a king.

[And what rule is equal, if you make Love the judge, to the glory of ruling in your heart?

ROB. And yet, when you see the gleam of the golden scepter and of the purple cloak flash upon your eyes, that flame which now kindles you for me will seem dull to you; and, when you think that you bear a crownèd head, you will despise even the name of Roberto.

[COST. I pardon these sweet insults because of your love. I call Heaven and the gods all to witness here . . .

ROB. Ah, be silent! With your new rank you will change your ideas and your ways.

COST. You do not know my heart well, and yet you possess it all. Let us escape now, if you wish, to where there is less risk and more peace; I will follow your steps wherever you wish.

ROB. No, no. Reign in the world as you do in my heart. I am not so base as to urge you to come down from the throne. I would not love you, if I loved you at such cost.

COST. Remember that if I am wed to another husband, you will have to leave my side and my heart forever, and honor and faithfulness will forbid me even to look at you, for your punishment and mine.

ROB. I know this; but I still desire greatness for you more than pleasure for myself.

17 COST. Fair countenance, you still do not know what sorrow you will experience, losing a beauty who loves you so much. If you see me belonging to someone else, then you will weep; but it will then be futile to dissolve in tears. Fair countenance, etc.

Scene viii

GUALTIERO *with numerous followers,* CORRADO, OTTONE, *and* ROBERTO

18 GUAL. (*Aside to* CORRADO) Keep the secret to yourself.

CORR. My straightforward faithfulness is quite well known to you.

GUAL. Meanwhile flatter Costanza's desire some, and grant her some hope. In a short time she will know that she is my daughter, and that I am receiving her with the affection of a father, and not that of a husband.

CORR. Here, Sire, is my brother. He has accompanied the royal bride with me.

GUAL. My belovèd Roberto . . . (*in the act of embracing him*). But where is Costanza?

ROB. She just now went towards that fountain.

GUAL. Ottone, tell her that I am longing for her.

OTT. I am at my Queen's service. (*Exit.*)

CORR. (*Aside, as above*) And what has happened to Griselda?

GUAL. To my great sorrow, I pretended to reject her, so that the pride of this unwise people should learn what virtue and what courage shine in her. (*Sees* COSTANZA *returning*) But! . . . is that she?

CORR. It is; now tell me whether a fairer ideal ever came down to earth from the sphere of Love?

GUAL. (*Enter* COSTANZA.) Fair Costanza, how glad I am to meet you; and what tenderness and happiness, children of love, I feel on embracing you!

COST. My lord, my soul, taken aback at your royal graciousness, answers with silence; and when it is silent, it is most expressive of its timid affections.

ROB. (Suffer, o my wretched heart!)

CORR. (My brother is sad.)

GUAL. Come now, my belovèd, come and enjoy part of a palace with me, which Heaven has prepared for you since you were in the cradle. You too will come, Roberto, o worthy scion of a royal stock; let my palace receive ornament from you, and my kingdom joy.

ROB. Great King, you do me too much honor.

GUAL. Ottone!

OTT. My renowned lord?

GUAL. If Griselda has not yet left the royal dwelling, have her leave it immediately, so as to place no obstacle in the way of my happiness.

OTT. I carry out your command. (*Exit.*)

GUAL. But you seem sad to me; you are timid and silent, and your eyes never meet mine.

CORR. Grant, o lord, this unintentional error to the maidenly blushes of a tender girl.
You know that honest beauty is more accustomed to remain silent than to speak.]

GUAL. Until the fair damsel overcomes her fear, let her not be separated from you. Escort her to the palace. You, Roberto, wait upon her; and you, Corrado, tell her, as you know full well, that I loved her even before seeing her.
You are fair, o amorous countenance; but those 19 attractive lips of yours seem to wish to sigh. Have no fear, o crimson mouth; I come to embrace you as a bride and as a daughter. You are fair, etc.

Scene ix

CORRADO, ROBERTO, COSTANZA, *and their retinue*

ROB. As a concession to my rejoicing, allow me to 20 reverently press kisses of faithfulness on your white hand, now that it is so near to holding the weight of the bejewelled scepter.

COST. Roberto, your happiness is not the first proof that you have given me of your devotion; you have often urgèd me to reign, and often to that throne, where I have arrived, you have raised me with your wishes.

CORR. Delay no longer; Gualtiero is perhaps impatiently complaining of your slowness.

COST.
ROB. } (Pretend, and torture yourself thus, poor heart!)

21 COST. Rejoice, fair soul, rejoice. (*To* ROBERTO) Be happy, console yourself, since my greatness is your happiness. You wanted me to be a queen, you made me a queen; Heaven will reward you for your zeal. Rejoice, etc.

Scene x
CORRADO *and* ROBERTO

22 ROB. Ah, Corrado, ah, my brother, if the fair Costanza was not to be mine, could not be mine, why, from my earliest years, did you not forbid me to love her? Why flatter my hopes in this way? Why betray my desires? Cruel one, I know full well that you would weep for your deceit, if you could see, o Heavens, the torture of my heart.

CORR. Roberto, our destinies take shape in Heaven before they do on earth, and it is forbidden for us to foresee them. But it still happens, that good often has the appearance of evil. Control your grief, and do not be so saddened; and remember that weeping often precedes true happiness.

ROB. Costanza was the only delight of my days; I have lost her. I may not ever hope for any other love, any other happiness ever again.

CORR. Roberto, before the day is over, you will be happy.

Scene xi
ROBERTO

23 ROB. What nonsense is this? What deceit? My loss is by now so obvious, that to doubt it would be the wanderings of a deranged mind. Unfortunately, my fair lady was pleasing to the king's glance. And who can ever see and not love such attractive eyes?

24 I might wish not to know you, o fair flattering eyes, so as not to be tortured so. But now that I am in such torture, do not be haughty; do you not betray me, even if Fate has betrayed me. I might wish, etc.

Scene xii

Aristocratic antechamber, with entry to the royal apartments, visible beyond. GRISELDA, *in shepherdess' garb, barred on the threshold by some guards.*

25 GRIS. And did Gualtiero order that I leave this threshold, chased off in this way?

And does he want me to go away without speaking to him or seeing him again?

(*To one of the guards*) O Heavens, Alceste, I cannot leave without life, without soul. I shall wait here for Gualtiero. You go, and, if my misfortune awakes in you a spark of pity, bring me my son, so that I may press on those tender lips, as a last comfort for my great sorrow, a single kiss.

Scene xiii
GRISELDA, *and* GUALTIERO *with retinue*

26 GUAL. What! Are you still in the palace, Griselda? You have not left?

GRIS. I am leaving, my belovèd king—since I may no longer say "my belovèd spouse." I am going back

to the forests; here I am, clothed in that rustic garb which pleased you.

GUAL. (How much grace and light does even distress add to her face!)

GRIS. I come in this guise before you, not expecting to please you now as well; if you loved me then, it was your kindness, not any merit of mine. I come only to receive the last look—be it pitying or cruel, it is still yours—from those eyes which are the belovèd and sweet flame on account of which I am enkindled.

GUAL. What? You are talking to me about yourself? I believed that my new bride was uppermost in your thoughts. I have seen her; how beautiful and noble! You yourself would love her, Griselda.

GRIS. I love her too; what is pleasing to your affections, is dear to mine.

GUAL. I want you to see the arrow with which my heart is sweetly pierced.

GRIS. Your happiness is a comfort to my sorrow.

GUAL. Admire her in this. (*Gives her a picture of* COSTANZA.)

GRIS. O Heavens! What a likeness! What a face!

GUAL. What do you think of her?

GRIS. O my lord, in her eyes she has your eyes, in her brow she has yours, and in her I see, only somewhat less firm, your face.

GUAL. Is she beautiful?

GRIS. She is worthy of you.

GUAL. I shall enjoy happiness with her. (*Takes the picture from her hand.*)

GRIS. May Heaven grant you, with so sweet a companion, a long life, an auspicious reign. May the grandchildren of your children play around you, and, from time to time in such a series of lofty good fortunes, may you barely remember your wretched, faithful Griselda.

GUAL. Have you anything further to say?

GRIS. May you keep the pity which you deny me, for your innocent son, and in him pardon, not my, but your blood.

GUAL. No more!

GRIS. I am leaving, Sire. I have kept you here too long, far from the object of your love; I can see on your brow the effort you are making.

GUAL. Return to the forests, and make haste, for I am going back to admire my belovèd.

What fair tyranny, what sweet enchantment has 27 this heart of mine found in two eyes! (*Aside, seeing* GRISELDA *weep*) (Be still, o my fair one, dry your tears; for I am already all ablaze on seeing your weeping.) What fair, etc.

Scene xiv

GRISELDA, *to whom* EVERARDO *is brought; later* OTTONE.

GRIS. Everardo (*going towards and embracing her* 28 *son*), o sweet fruit of my love, even in you I kiss a part of this soul; I kiss the adored image of my Gualtiero, and in a single slow kiss I feel the intensity of my torture become less.

OTT. (How opportunely I have arrived!)

GRIS. Belovèd cheeks, and dear . . .

OTT. To me, Griselda. (*Takes the boy away from her suddenly.*)

GRIS. Who is so pitiless in heart that he denies a last unhappy embrace to a mother and her child?

OTT. Your Gualtiero, your Gualtiero himself.

GRIS. From more hated lips a more belovèd name could not come to my ears.

OTT. I, if you wish it, shall take pity and give your belovèd son back to you, even despite the King.

GRIS. I refuse the gift!

OTT. Ungrateful woman!

GRIS. And swiftly, to escape the sight of you, I already hasten my feet for the fatal departure.

OTT. Stop!

GRIS. What do you wish?

OTT. That for just one minute, o fair lady . . .

29 GRIS. My heart has already understood your speech. Say that it is a dream, or delirium, if I ever say that I love you. And if I ever turn my glance on you less disdainfully, say that my anger is hidden in my bosom, but not that it has been appeased. Say, etc.

Scene xv
OTTONE, *with* EVERARDO, *who is then taken away.*

30 OTT. With such a refractory beauty prayers and charms are futile efforts. I shall try a different way, and I am already planning it. Let my art and my skill be put to use; for without some trickery, he who is spurned in love never has enjoyment.

31 That tyrant who wounds my heart seems to me so fair because she is contemptuous, because she is pitiless. I should like to appease her, but I do not know whether her eyes will be so beautiful when she is appeased. That tyrant, etc.

Scene xvi
Royal quarters, elegantly prepared for COSTANZA. *Table on one side, with mantle, crown, and scepter.* CORRADO *and* COSTANZA.

32 CORR. These rooms which you behold are your royal apartments.

COST. The price of several kingdoms is collected here in a small space.

CORR. Griselda also had her abode here for a time.

COST. The one of whom I heard you speak so often, a nymph and a queen?

CORR. You see there her mantle, her crown, and her scepter.

COST. And now in the woods . . .

CORR. . . . disconsolate and wandering . . .

COST. . . . she wears, in her task, base rough woollens . . .

CROR. . . . and of Gualtiero's heart . . .

COST. . . . to whom she was so dear for her beauty and faithfulness . . .

CORR. . . . she leaves you as heiress.

COST. Poor woman!

CORR. Pity is the daughter of a noble soul. But with

what kind of love do you requite Gualtiero's?

COST. With that which is suitable for a bride.

CORR. And that for a lover, for whom do you keep it? That is the most tender affection.

COST. Alas!

CORR. Do not blush; more than Gualtiero, you love Roberto.

COST. O Heavens! I loved him first with your heart, then with mine.

CORR. And now?

COST. I have for my bridegroom fear and respect. I bow before his rank, I honor his crown, I respect his throne; and I adore Roberto alone!

CORR. Here he comes.

COST. How lost in thought he is! I shall avoid his presence.

CORR. Stay and hear him.

COST. I am a bride.

CORR. You have not yet sworn the faith of a spouse.

COST. Ah, honor forbids me.

CORR. And love demands it of you.

Scene xvii
COSTANZA, *then* ROBERTO

33 COST. Before I cease loving you, o my belovèd sweetheart, I shall cease living; but here, let my sufferings be salved by pretending cruelty towards his.

ROB. Costanza? Alas, what do I see? You turn away? You avoid me? And you are silent? And you begrudge me the wretched delight even of a glance?

COST. My rank disdains love, and commands respect.

ROB. (O my heart, there is no more hope.)

COST. Have you heard?

ROB. I have heard, o Queen.

COST. Now what do you desire?

ROB. To prostrate myself at your feet an instant, and to speak to you.

COST. Anything else?

ROB. Nothing more.

COST. Respect my rank, and depart.

ROB. I shall obey; but first tell me by what strength of character, or by what magic, you have already forgotten . . .

COST. As a queen and a wife, you see full well, Roberto, that I may listen to none other, I may love none other than the king, my spouse.

ROB. (Ah, unhappy Roberto!)

34 COST. (If only Gualtiero were at least so charming!) You sigh, o belovèd charms; I know it, I see it, and I am filled with pity. But I too sigh too much, o Heavens, not to shield myself with cruelty. You, etc.

Scene xviii
ROBERTO

35 ROB. Who ever saw a fate like mine? Love cast my belovèd into my arms. When I was already almost clasping her and almost enjoying possession of her, in a flash he tore her from me, he snatched her from my bosom! In my tortured sorrow, the loss torments

me, and the deceit still more.

36 Ye lovers who weep, dry your tears and be consoled. For all loving hearts I alone will suffer, I alone will weep; you be happy. Ye lovers, etc.

END OF ACT I

ACT II

Scene i

Countryside with rustic dwelling, grove, hill and water-fall. GRISELDA

37 GRIS. You see me again, o shady wood, but no longer as a queen or spouse. You see me again as an unfortunate, despised shepherdess. This is indeed my paternal mountain, this is my belovèd spring, this my meadow, and this the brook; but I alone am not the same. You see me again, etc.

Here is the occasion for the soul to furnish proof of itself. If it was able to don the royal garb without pride, now let it be able to return to its earlier poverty without baseness. Gualtiero, Gualtiero alone troubles my firm resolve; only in the memory of my lost belovèd do I feel my misfortunes and my sorrows.

Scene ii

OTTONE *and* GRISELDA

38 OTT. Griselda, my soul.
GRIS. Even in the forests do you still come, Ottone, to trouble me?
OTT. I am coming in search of the heart which you have taken from me.
GRIS. You know that I want no love.
OTT. You may wish for no lover, but not for no love. How can you avoid being loved?
GRIS. I shall repel with disdain others' empty flattery.
OTT. And with your disdain you will make yourself more lovable and more belovèd.
GRIS. Leave me alone, Ottone.
OTT. Your fair eyes war too fiercely on me.
GRIS. After all, what do you want of me?
OTT. That reward which is due to my affection and my faithfulness.
GRIS. Base man!
OTT. What? Am I asking you for a reward which is a crime? With your rejection, you have become free again from your marital bonds; I am offering you another no less chaste, and more dependable. Even in a rustic shift, even slandered and neglected in the forest, I want you for my wife; and even if I do not have a king's crown on my head, I count many kings among my ancestors, and over many lands I too have sovereign command.
GRIS. Ottone, farewell.
OTT. See, Griselda (*holding her back*), I am filling all the roles of a supplicant lover. Do not complain, if then you force me to be cruel.
39 A loving dove, belovèd of her dear lover, does not hate her faithful one and is not cruel to him, but says in her language "Love him who loves you." You too, o fair one, return love for love, and give your heart to him who yearns for you. A loving dove, etc.

Scene iii

GRISELDA, *then* CORRADO *with* EVERARDO *and guards.*
40 GRIS. I have only one soul in my bosom, only one heart, and this will belong to Gualtiero so long as I breathe.

But I feel I am weary from excessive effort. Come, Griselda, let us go to where the rustic bed, with bare straw, invites you to rest your weariness a little. There, accustom your sorrow to silence and peace, finally forgetting, not Gualtiero, but your royal greatness.
CORR. O fair unfortunate, restrain your footsteps and behold the gift which I bring you.
GRIS. (*Going towards* EVERARDO) O son! O gift!
CORR. I am here to carry out a cruel order.
GRIS. Speak, for the import of my woes is already known to me.
CORR. Gualtiero has commanded . . .
GRIS. . . . that my tender son should be a companion to me in my harsh exile.
CORR. Your fate has no such mercy.
GRIS. Heavens, what can it ever be?
CORR. Where the forest is most dense and fearful, there I am to expose your Everardo to the wild beasts.
GRIS. Have you any more arrows, o Fortune, to discharge at my head? And you, cruel man, do you come to me with so fine a gift?
CORR. Read, o noble-spirited lady, my sorrow in my face; but I must carry out my orders.
GRIS. Ah, whoever you may be, if you have any spirit of humanity in your bosom, if ever you enjoyed the sweet name of father, or if you ever yearned for it, hear and pity the prayers and sighs of a wretched mother. Give me my son.
CORR. I fear that I will be merciful to you with danger to myself.
GRIS. I will hide him; I will take him where the determined harshness of my fate will not find or reach him.
CORR. You move me to pity. Take him, and let him be your care. (*Gives her the child.*) Let his misfortune not fall on my head.
GRIS. Let this tender weeping, begotten of my joy, give thanks to you for me.
CORR. Dry, o fair lady, and calm your beautiful eyes. I hope that one day your virtue will defeat your ill-fortune, and, almost, my heart foretells that you will not always be an unhappy mother.
41 Shaken by a violent storm, a rose, which among the roses seemed a star, was languishing in that field. But when that fatal cloud had cleared, she returned to her regal pride, and, garbed in purple and gold, she shone even more lofty and beautiful. Shaken, etc.

Scene iv

GRISELDA, *with* EVERARDO; *then* OTTONE, *with a bare sword, and followers.*

42 GRIS. Son, where shall I hide you from an ungrateful father, who is trying to destroy his own image in your fair face, and in your sweet love the memory of me?

Alas, there remains, out of a whole kingdom which a short while ago was mine, no place where I can hide a boy, where he can breathe the air of my sighs!

OTT. You do not yet know all of your fate, o woman.

GRIS. I expect from Ottone nothing but evil. What do you bring?

OTT. In this sword, death to Everardo.

GRIS. My soul, if you resist your sorrow, you are stupid, not strong.

OTT. (*To one of his followers*) Come, Araspe, and listen to me. After you have opened the way out for this soul, by several paths, take the shapeless corpse, cut it into many pieces, and throw it, as tender bits of food for the beasts, where the wood is darkest.

GRIS. Ah, Ottone . . .

OTT. You resist in vain.

GRIS. Unfortunate child, in what have you sinned?

OTT. (*To the soldiers*) Make haste.

GRIS. (*Prostrating herself*) Ah, Prince!

OTT. Woman, what do you want?

GRIS. She who is prostrate before you and begs you humbly is a mother.

OTT. To her who refuses pity, pity is refused.

GRIS. Leave me my dear son, and if I have offended you, take me for your victim.

OTT. Make up your mind; either marry me, or I kill him.

GRIS. (*Looking at* EVERARDO) The unfortunate innocent has his little eyes fixed on me, and knows nothing of his misfortune!

OTT. Griselda, if you delay any more, you will no longer be a mother. I am already measuring off the blow which Gualtiero has ordered.

GRIS. (*Unjust father!*)

OTT. And I am already carrying out the cruel sentence which you yourself are confirming.

GRIS. I?

OTT. With your refusal.

GRIS. And do my tears not move you?

OTT. Let them sink into the sand.

GRIS. Nor do my prayers move you?

OTT. Let the winds scatter them.

GRIS. Nor does my blood appease you?

OTT. I want that which flows in the veins of your Everardo.

GRIS. Gualtiero . . . ?

OTT. This is his command.

GRIS. Ottone . . . ?

OTT. . . . is to be his executant.

GRIS. Heaven . . . ?

OTT. . . . does not defend you.

GRIS. God . . .

OTT. . . . is deaf.

GRIS. And by giving you my hand . . .

OTT. . . . the mother can save her child, the bride can appease her lover, and disarm the hand of its unsheathed sword.

GRIS. Obey your king. Kill him, cruel man! (*She leaves the boy to him, and starts out firmly. Then, on the point of leaving, she stops at the call of* OTTONE *who is in the act of striking* EVERARDO.)

OTT. Stony-hearted mother, see with what rage I sink my steel in your vitals. Behold, I am striking now.

GRIS. Ah, sorrow and fright restrain me, and I try in vain to flee, half alive, from this horrible and fatal tragedy. (*Comes back.*)

Son? Tyrant? (*First to one and then to the other*) 43 Oh Heavens? Tell me, what can I do? Son? Tyrant? The love of a loving mother pierces my heart in my bosom; but the too steadfast heart, even so pierced, overcomes its torment. Son, etc.

Scene v

OTTONE, *with* EVERARDO *and his followers*

OTT. Flattery, threats, deceit are of no use. What am 44 I to do? Ungrateful woman, let force finally avail with you, and make you mine.

I shall carry you off. But perhaps Gualtiero will be angry at this. Nay, Gualtiero, free of the obstacle of an abhorred and rejected wife, will consider my crime his good fortune. To work, therefore, and meanwhile let this child remain under guard. He has my cruel enemy in his face; let him be the first laurel of my victory.

Pitiless beauty, in spite of yourself I desire to ac- 45 quire you; and a heart which you hate, with fierce delight I desire to give you. Pitiless beauty, etc.

Scene vi

Great Gallery. ROBERTO *and* COSTANZA

ROB. So you love me no longer. 46

COST. You have already understood me.

ROB. Is it possible?

COST. I have made myself sufficiently plain to you.

ROB. (What faithless beauty!)

COST. (What fair eyes!)

ROB. Although a serious fire can be put out, it always leaves some sparks which burn for some time and go out only gradually.

COST. I have put out entirely the first fire in my heart.

ROB. Do you perhaps love Gualtiero?

COST. What am I to say? I feel something strange in my heart; perhaps it is not, but it seems like a new love.

ROB. I am glad that your spirit and your desire is beginning to be happy with your new spouse.

COST. Since you are glad of it, I am glad too.

I wish to make you happy, o unfurrowed brow. I want to fall in love with that countenance. Oh, how I shall laugh at your sorrow, when I shall be happy with my new lover. I wish, etc.

(*Starts to leave, but* ROBERTO *holds her back.*)

ROB. Where are you fleeing to, cruel girl?

COST. What do you want of me? Was it not your command that I should be unfaithful to you?

ROB. It is true; but you could have accomplished my desire, since I expressed it, with more tenderness and less haughtiness, stealing from your bridegroom and giving my sorrow a caress, an encouragement, a single sigh; thus . . .

COST. Be silent, ungrateful man; you deserve no pity.

ROB. You see that I too can be disdainful.

COST. And then?

ROB. I can, if I wish, return haughtiness for haughtiness, pride for pride, disdain for disdain, and avenge myself.

COST. What? Are you thinking of leaving me?

ROB. And you, do you think that I cannot give my affections to some beauty more noble and perhaps even more faithful and constant than you?

COST. Pitiless man, could you do this?

ROB. Do you not know it?

COST. Does sorrow make you go so far?

ROB. Sorrow and love.

COST. Go; I do not care.

47 ROB. You do not understand what a torment jealousy is, because I adore you faithfully. But perhaps you will understand it, when you see that I love another beauty. You do not, etc.

Scene vii
GUALTIERO, ROBERTO, and COSTANZA

48 GUAL. Where are you going Roberto? I would like you to be with me.

ROB. My King . . .

GUAL. What was the charming Costanza saying to you?

ROB. She, my lord, is always speaking of the love she has for you.

GUAL. Can I believe this, fair lady?

COST. Roberto knows it.

GUAL. Yet you do not show me all the grace of your countenance; and it seems to me that I see on your white cheek and your red lip the rose but half alive in the arms of the lily.

COST. Nothing is troubling me, my lord.

ROB. She is afflicted only by your absence.

GUAL. On this day the pomp of the happy wedding will be resplendent. I want you to come with me, for sport and pleasure, hunting wild animals there in the royal forest.

COST. This soul accepts humbly the sovereign honor.

GUAL. (To COSTANZA) Roberto too is to accompany me.

ROB. A favor which exceeds my deserts.

GUAL. (To ROBERTO) Thus it will happen that perhaps laughter will return to her sweet face amid the pearly tears.

49 (To COSTANZA) My beautiful light, you are not happy; I see full well that something afflicts you. That blush of yours tells my heart that your heart is not at rest. My beautiful, etc.

Scene viii
ROBERTO and COSTANZA

50 COST. You will be satisfied, Roberto; today you will see your wishes fulfilled. Today Gualtiero . . . what are you doing? (Goes and looks in his face.) What tears are these? Where is your great heart which, undaunted, wished greatness for me? Do you change like this? You have not yet lost me, and are already weeping for me?

51 ROB. If I wish for you to be another's, my beautiful idol, be angry, not with me, but with Love. He who loves you, and gives you up to give you a crown, is cruel, not to you, but to his own heart. If I wish, etc.

Scene ix
COSTANZA

52 COST. Yes, I am angry with Love—with Love which betrays such fair hopes; with Love, which gives such a cruel, wicked reward to so many sighs and so much faithfulness.

53 Sometimes tyrannical Love catches a heart in his snares, he entices it on, and flatters it, but then he makes a slaughter of it. Like a charming boy, who, if he catches a bird, caresses it and then kills it. Sometimes, etc.

Scene x
A part of the forest with various pathways, and the sea in the distance. On one side, GRISELDA's shepherdess' hut, seen open with rustic bed, and other huts nearby.

54 GRIS. Is it weakness of heart or weariness of weeping which now overcomes you, o my eyes? It is not sleep, for you no longer are accustomed to quiet rest. But if it is indeed sleep, coming to rest me in spite of my woes, let it be eternal sleep. (*Sits on the bed.*)

55 The pleasure you have in harming me, o cruel fate, will come to an end; you can rob me only of myself, for I have nothing more to lose. You have deprived me of my children and my spouse and my realm; you have left me only my life, and this too I will give you. The pleasure, etc.

56 (*She falls asleep. The Royal Hunt meanwhile continues.*)

Scene xi
GRISELDA *asleep in the hut.* COSTANZA, *and later* ROBERTO

COST. Hear, hear, o empty forests, what a strange trouble I feel in my heart. It is pain and delight, pride and affection, fear and hope, and has the appearance of disdain and love. Hear, etc.†

57 ROB. In these deserted haunts, are you perhaps hiding from me?

†This aria was later replaced by a different one on a similar text: "Hear, o friendly plants, the sorrow of a loving soul, which is and, together with my heart, becomes sweet hope and cruelty." It is not certain whether music for either or both of these aria texts was ever composed; no music is found in any of the sources.

282

COST. While the king enjoys wandering through these shady trees on the track of either a timid hare or a fleeting doe, I am waiting for him, weary, where he told me to.

ROB. And, in your brief stay, you are ennobling these wild huts as much as any lofty palace.

COST. Now that the plain and the mountain re-echo with barkings and shouts, you alone, Roberto, are not eager for prey; and you alone are not following the king, my bridegroom.

ROB. I am following you, my fair lady; and if you were my sweet prey . . .

COST. Be still, and go with the others where Gualtiero is.

ROB. Why must I leave you?

COST. In such out-of-the-way regions I do not want you by my side.

ROB. Of what are you afraid?

COST. I am afraid for my reputation; the king might become suspicious or jealous.

ROB. Are you still angry at me? Do you still turn your adored glance on me in disdain or refusal or unwillingness?

58

Peace, beautiful eyes, peace with my soul, belovèd eyes. If the wounds you cause in peace are so many, how many must they be when you are disdainful? Peace, etc.

Scene xii
COSTANZA, *and* GRISELDA *asleep*

59 COST. Even if you go away, Roberto, I am not alone; even in this humble hut . . . (*Starting to enter the hut, she sees* GRISELDA.) What do I see? A woman seated on the bed, asleep and weeping! (*Goes up to her.*) How noble her face is! Her coarse and humble garb does not cover its light, nor her beauty! I feel, on beholding her, a strange movement in my soul; my blood stirs in my veins, and my heart pounds in my bosom!

GRIS. (*Asleep*) Come!

COST. She opens her arms to me, and, while sleeping still, invites me to her sweet embrace. My heart advises me; I can no longer resist. (*Runs and embraces her.*)

GRIS. Belovèd daughter! (*Awakes*) Alas!

COST. Have no fear, o nymph. (The most beautiful part of her face she has revealed in her eyes!)

GRIS. (Heavens! Am I really awake? Or are my thoughts deceiving me?)

COST. (How attentively she is looking at me!)

GRIS. By her lips, by her eyelashes, by the air of her face I recognize her; it is she. I have kept her appearance too firmly imprinted on my heart.

COST. Do not be amazed any longer.

GRIS. And what fate has brought you to this crude dwelling, o royal lady (for such I believe you to be)?

COST. Weary of following my spouse in the hunt, I came here to rest.

GRIS. This is the dwelling-place of sorrow, not of rest.

COST. If you are willing, you will be comforted in your misfortunes by Costanza.

GRIS. Is that your name?

COST. Exactly.

GRIS. A daughter of mine, who was killed, was named Costanza too.

COST. Poor mother!

GRIS. Blame my heart, if I am asking too much. Where were you born?

COST. Ah, where I have lived, I know, but not where I was born.

GRIS. Your fatherland . . . ?

COST. . . . is unknown to me.

GRIS. Your parents . . . ?

COST. Heaven has hidden them from me.

GRIS. And you know nothing for certain about yourself?

COST. Only that I am the daughter of a king.

GRIS. Who has brought you up?

COST. Corrado, who holds the scepter of Apulia.

GRIS. And your spouse?

COST. He is Gualtiero who rules over Sicily.

GRIS. You are indeed worthy of him. My dream deceived me! (I thought I would press my daughter in a tender embrace and I embrace my rival!)

COST. What dream?

GRIS. I thought, a short time ago, I was embracing my dead daughter in my sleep, and I was weeping with joy.

COST. Ah, if you were the mother . . .

GRIS. Ah, if you were the daughter . . .

COST. . . . whom I am seeking . . .

GRIS. . . . of whom I am dreaming . . .

COST. . . . but if I am the daughter of a king . . .

GRIS. . . . but if an evil star brought death upon her . . .

COST. . . . I know, kind nymph . . . ⎫
GRIS. . . . I know, royal bride . . . ⎭ you are not the one.

BOTH. You are not the one, and yet my heart tells my heart that you are. 60

COST. Beautiful eyes . . . ⎫
GRIS. Belovèd lips . . . ⎭ in you I see . . .

COST. . . . that mother whom I am sighing for.

GRIS. . . . that daughter whom I lost.
You are not, etc.

Scene xiii
GUALTIERO, COSTANZA, *and* GRISELDA

GUAL. This rustic roof is unworthy of your fair eyes, my dear. 61

COST. Its kind inhabitant makes it noble and worthy.

GUAL. Do you come here, too, to torment me, woman?

GRIS. My King, it is not my fault; this is my former humble dwelling.

GUAL. Do not call me your king any more, but your enemy.

COST. If my prayers are worthy of your favor . . .

GUAL. And what power does Costanza not have over this heart?

COST. . . . grant that she no longer leave my side; in

the palace, in the woods, wherever I may dwell, let her be my companion or servant.

GUAL. She, a servant to you? Do you know who she is?

COST. If I judge by her clothes, she is base; if by her bearing, noble.

GUAL. You are looking now at the one who was my consort, whom I loved to my undoing, when she was raised to the throne, to be an eternal disgrace to it.

GRIS. O Heavens!

GUAL. She, who made her baseness and my love known to the world.

COST. Griselda?

GUAL. Ah, do not say it again; to my lips, too, came the abhorred name, and yet I repressed it. A baser wife . . .

GRIS. (. . . and a more faithful one . . .)

GUAL. . . . was never born.

COST. Even though she may be base or lowly, an incomprehensible love, with an unknown force, attracts me to her.

GUAL. What a difficult bond!

COST. And even rarer in friendship.

GRIS. (I must prepare my heart to endure still more.)

Scene xiv
CORRADO *with his retinue, and the aforementioned*

62   CORR. I have heard from a trustworthy scout, Sire, that Ottone, armed, is coming towards this hill at the head of armed troops. I therefore have come hither immediately, with your faithful men.

GUAL. Ottone armed? and for what purpose, o Prince?

CORR. To kidnap Griselda, and in a few minutes.

COST. Against this mad daring let the king's disdain take arms.

CORR. And let Ottone, the base kidnapper, die.

GUAL. No, no. Let every one of you give way. What do I care, if Griselda is kidnapped? Let Fortune decide as she will. Let Ottone kidnap her.

CORR. Such harshness?

GUAL. I wish it thus.

COST. And I . . .

GUAL. Abandon her to her fate!

COST. Your lord and mine is too cruel. (*Exit with the others.*)

GRIS. And is it true . . . ?

GUAL. Go away.

GRIS. Do not allow anyone else, in such an outcome, to take away from you the honor of killing me.

63   GUAL. You would like, by your weeping, to arouse my pity; but my pleasure comes from your sorrow. It shall be my glory and boast to be cruel to you, since having once loved you was my shame. You would like, etc.

Scene xv
GRISELDA, *then* OTTONE

64   GRIS. Here is Ottone. Alone, unarmed, what can I do? Let at least my arrow be my defense. (*Goes and takes her arrow, left on the bed.*)

OTT. Do you defend yourself against him who adores you, my fair lady?

GRIS. Come on, come, unjust man, and after the son kill the mother too.

OTT. I love Everardo, and shall love him as a father.

GRIS. So he is still living?

OTT. And you too shall live with him, Griselda, and shall be mine. Follow me.

GRIS. I will not listen to you.

OTT. Come.

GRIS. I would a thousand times rather go to my tomb.

OTT. And what do you expect to do?

GRIS. As much as a desperate and strong soul can do; to give you, or to receive, death.

OTT. Now we shall see.

GRIS. To one side, or I shall plunge this arrow into your heart.

OTT. Fair lady, with one glance of yours Love has aleady dealt it a mortal blow.

GRIS. My right hand will know how to follow my eyes.

OTT. It is futile to resist any longer; make up your mind, and do not insist on making me guilty of a greater misdeed.

GRIS. I have no fear of violence.

OTT. Ho there, my trusty men! (*Enter armed men.*)

GRIS. Woe is me! Aid! Help!

OTT. Take her where I told you to. It is the king's command.

Scene xvi
GUALTIERO *with his guards,* CORRADO, COSTANZA, *and the aforementioned*

GUAL. It is the king's command? You are too faithful,   65 Ottone.

OTT. (The king! Cruel fate!) (OTTONE's *men withdraw.*)

GUAL. It is a faithful vassal's duty to make the deed come before the order. It is not just that I should leave your zeal unrewarded.

GRIS. (Heaven has always protected the innocent.)

GUAL. Corrado, let Ottone be escorted to my palace.

CORR. He will have me as a faithful guardian.

GUAL. In a friendly dwelling, Ottone, it is useless to gird on your sword; you can leave it in my hands.

OTT. Here it is at your feet. (Inhuman fate!) (*Part of the guards go with* OTTONE *and* CORRADO.)

Scene xvii
GUALTIERO, GRISELDA, *and* COSTANZA

GRIS. What thanks can I . . .   66

GUAL. Give them to Costanza's pity, not mine; your safety is a favor from her, not from me.

GRIS. (*To* COSTANZA) An unhappy life, since it is dear to you, even Griselda values.

COST. Complete the gift, Sire. Now let Griselda, taken from the forest again, come with me to the palace.

GUAL. And let her come as a servant where she lived as queen.

GRIS. I shall come as a handmaiden and slave.

GUAL. There, you are to fulfill and observe all the duties of the basest service, and, not complaining, accustom your haughty soul to the function of a servant.

COST. Have no fear, my belovèd; you will follow me with the name of sister or mother. Undivided from my side, at daybreak or dusk, you will embrace me, I shall embrace you. Often you will look at yourself in my eyes, and I shall admire, in your beautiful face, my own.

67 GUAL. (*To* GRISELDA) I shall always hate you.

COST. (*To* GRISELDA) I shall always love you.

GRIS. And I shall know how to live always faithful, and to live and die for you (*to* GUALTIERO) and for you (*to* COSTANZA).

GUAL. (*To* GRISELDA) I shall always be cruel . . .

COST. (*To* GRISELDA) I shall always be loving . . .

BOTH. . . . when I behold your countenance.

GRIS. And I shall always be constant (*to* GUALTIERO) and loving (*to* COSTANZA) to you (*to* GUALTIERO) and you (*to* COSTANZA).

GUAL. I shall, etc.

END OF ACT II

ACT III

Scene i

Royal rooms with small throne. GRISELDA, *and* OTTONE *with guards, from different sides.*

68 GRIS. Treacherous man, I wanted to have you where you have come to be. I shall see your boldness finally punished by your death.

OTT. Such fierceness in so beautiful a bosom?

GRIS. Unjust man, I want you dead.

OTT. In such a charming mouth, such thirst for blood?

GRIS. Your crimes . . .

OTT. My crimes, o fair lady, are nothing else than a great love. I strayed from the path of virtue only because I love you, and because I love you greatly.

GRIS. Do you call violence, betrayal, kidnapping "excesses of love," you unworthy man?

OTT. Calm your tender disdain, and in your own beauty recognize the source of all my guilt. I would be more innocent if you were less beautiful and more merciful.

GRIS. But what have you done with my son, cruel man? Where is he? Have you killed him?

OTT. I, kill such a belovèd token of affection? and how? with kisses, perhaps? To his father, who loves him, to his father, who is sighing and calling for him, my faithful Araspe is giving him back right now.

GRIS. If you are lying . . .

OTT. I shall pay for my lie with my life.

GRIS. Ottone, farewell; I have pity for your sufferings.

OTT. And for my love?

GRIS. You are making me to be troubled, and to live without soul, without heart.

69 OTT. I understand you, fair lips; I understand you, fair eyes; do you want me to die? Let me go and die. But while I am leaving, but while I am dying, o fair eyes of love, cast a glance on me; fair attractive lips, cast a sigh. I understand you, etc.

Scene ii

GRISELDA *and* COSTANZA

COST. Come and clasp me to your bosom, my sweet 70 companion. Next to my spouse, you are the tenderest love of this heart.

GRIS. And you are, my belovèd, the only possession that fate, in the midst of so many woes, has left me.

COST. How afflicted you are, my dear, on seeing that I am taking from you, through no fault of mine, your husband, and that through the power of Fate, when least I would wish it, I am your rival?

GRIS. I am so happy, fair girl, at your fate, that I do not think of mine.

COST. Perhaps one day jealousy, with its poison, will disturb the peace of your fair bosom.

GRIS. My greatest happiness is that Gualtiero should love you and that you should love him; and I shall be all the more happy if you love him as much as I loved him.

COST. What would you say, my faithful lady? Whether I love him or not, I am still not sure.

GRIS. Your innocence makes me love you still more. Love him, for he is worthy of it; and if ever, to love him with more strongly kindled desire, you need a heart, take mine.

Take mine, if you need a heart; and join my love 71 with your love. Thus you will be able to love so worthy a husband, as much as you want to, with the one and the other heart. Take, etc.

Scene iii

COSTANZA *and* ROBERTO

ROB. Could an unhappy prince, on such a beautiful 72 day, obtain a boon from a queen?

COST. Provided he not ask for love, he will obtain what he asks; I promise it.

ROB. The boon is small, and very far from love, in fact very different.

COST. He may have it.

ROB. To the promise, add your royal faith.

COST. The royal faith is pledged. Now what do you desire of me?

ROB. I am still hesitating, lest you scorn me and mock me.

COST. No, no; your fear is in vain.

ROB. Then here is the sword, here is my bosom; I want you to kill me.

COST. O Heaven! I cannot.

ROB. The authority of the royal promise safeguards my wishes. What are you thinking of? What are you worried about? Does a queen slander in such a way and disgrace her promised faith?

COST. I am not yet queen.

ROB. You are the bride of a great monarch; in this day, your fate already destines you to rule.

COST. I will kill you when I am queen.

ROB. You already are; I have already bought you this crown, and this throne which you will proudly mount today, at the price of my tears; I am seeking your glory, and you insult it?

COST. I cared nothing for this glory, ingrate. You, who esteem it so highly and love it so much, follow it as you will; from this glory you will obtain what you desire. Address your prayers to her; shower your charms on her; [call her your belovèd] say to her "my love, my goddess" and with amorous joy now embrace in this glory your bride.

73 ROB. Beautiful eyes, stars of love, I am showing you my heart wide open. Do you see it full of arrows and sparks? You, o beautiful eyes, inflicted these wounds; you, o dear glances, hurled these darts; you poured on my bosom these flames by the thousand. Beautiful eyes, etc.

Scene iv
COSTANZA, GUALTIERO *and guards*

74 GUAL. Let Ottone be brought to me. (*Exeunt some guards.*) You are the very one, fair lady, whom I was seeking.

COST. I come into my king's presence with respect.

GUAL. A rumor, which I believe daring and false, has spread to the effect that your beautiful spirit is agreeing to marry me with great sorrow; that, as an innocent girl with a still milk-white hand you have your affection, your vows, and your sighs to another object of your love; and that, led to a union with me by a tyrant's force, you have brought me a heart without heart, a soul without life and without love.

COST. My lord, I know nothing of this rumor. Let Corrado bear witness to you of my honesty and innocence.

GUAL. In addition to the Prince's assurance, I should like some surer proof.

COST. (Help me, o gods!)

GUAL. Tell me . . .

COST. (What am I to do?)

GUAL. . . . if I am far from you, are you unhappy? Are you sad?

COST. I am not wholly at peace.

GUAL. And then, if I am present, are you happy? Are you glad?

COST. I feel an indescribable joy.

GUAL. When alone, and conversing with yourself, do you sometimes mention my name?

COST. Often, and with sorrow too.

GUAL. These are all, my fair damsel, signs of a heart that loves me; go, for my love desires nothing else from you.

75 COST. An affection, which I still do not understand, makes me be troubled and joyful on your account. But the joy does not seem like joy, the trouble does not seem like trouble; I do not understand, nor see why. An affection, etc.

Scene v
GUALTIERO *and* OTTONE *among guards*

76 OTT. Here I am before my king.

GUAL. (*Sits.*) Ottone, a crime, when confessed, is diminished. A guilty man who denies or is silent commits a new crime, by lying or being in contempt. Speak to me freely, and make pardon come easier for your misdeed.

OTT. I fear you as a judge, whether you sit on a tribunal or a throne.

GUAL. Did you, a short while ago, dare to kidnap Griselda?

OTT. My lips, convicted, yield to the testimony of the guard.

GUAL. Where were you intending to take her when you had kidnapped her?

OTT. Where you would not have been able to get her back.

GUAL. Who gave you advice and encouragement in this deed?

OTT. Ah, Sire . . . (*kneels*)

GUAL. Rise, and answer me truly and honestly.

OTT. From my heart, more than from my lips, hear the truth. Heaven knows whether, when Griselda was seated on the throne as your wife and my queen, I looked on her with an eye which was not that of a vassal. I felt pity for her rejection and her woes; from pity, love was born, which, when disappointed and despised, used first flattery and then force.

GUAL. Do you love Griselda, then?

OTT. It was love alone which induced me to kidnap her.

GUAL. And did you not fear my royal displeasure?

OTT. In loving, Sire, what you once loved and now love no longer, how do I offend you?

GUAL. Ottone, from the king's affections those of the vassal take their law and guide. This is your crime.

OTT. The crimes of love are absolved by Love; you, too, loved.

GUAL. Let pardon for your error be given to your valor and to that of your ancestors, to the blood shed for my kingdom, and to your faithfulness.

OTT. Let the object of my love also be given.

GUAL. Griselda?

OTT. Ah, it is not fitting for a woman who was your queen and consort to wander in mountains and forests. Countermand your refusal, and allow me, as a spouse succeeding you, to love in her the earlier object of your affection.

GUAL. (*To the guards, rising*) Let Griselda be summoned hither. See whether I am not even more merciful than you ask. I swear, Ottone, I swear it on my crown, that when I marry Costanza you shall have Griselda.

OTT. Oh, what a boon! Oh, joy! Let me at your royal feet . . . (*starts to prostrate himself*).

GUAL. No; first wait for the boon to be granted, and then give thanks.

77 OTT. Your splendid gift shows me the greatness of your throne, the greatness of your heart. I do not know what more to desire; you have nothing more to give me, if you do not give the kingdom too. Your splendid gift, etc.

Scene vi
GUALTIERO, *later* GRISELDA, *guards.*

78 GUAL. Perhaps it was from his love that the complaints of the people originated and were stirred up. That is useful to know.

GRIS. I gladly obey your instructions, Sire.

GUAL. Griselda, at sunset I shall renew the desires which were dampened in my bosom by your rejection.

GRIS. (And which, alive in mine, preserve my faith.)

GUAL. You are to prepare their noble setting, clad, as you are, in coarse garb.

GRIS. (A maid-servant at that marriage-couch at which I was a bride.)

GUAL. You, guards, withdraw. (*Exeunt guards.*) This soul is impatient for the approaching joys, and chaste love is repining in inactivity.

GRIS. (Wretched woman, do you still not die?)

GUAL. You are too offensive, Griselda, to the general rejoicing, with your mournfulness. Restrain your sighs there, as an onlooker without sadness. I also forbid you the liberty of weeping, and I set a limit to your sorrow.

79 GRIS. To please you, I shall conceal it in my heart. If my sadness displeases you, here I am joyful in expression; here is a smile on my lips, here is joy in my bosom. I shall give a finer proof of my steadfast love by changing my sorrow into peaceful calm. If my, etc.

Scene vii
GUALTIERO

80 GUAL. I am troubled, but I am troubled for you, faithful wife, belovèd spouse; and while a cruel fate forces me to be an unjust tyrant towards you, in your heart and mine I feel your anguish. Ah, forgive me, my belovèd; only to make you happy am I making you unhappy; only because I love you, my soul, am I tormenting you.

81 I have in my bosom two flames, alike noble and beautiful: one is your beauty, the other is your worth. The affection of my bosom is divided between the two: I adore your fair countenance, and I adore your beautiful heart. I have, etc.

Scene viii
A side-lighted avenue in the royal gardens.
ROBERTO, *later* CORRADO.

82 ROB. As the bee goes from flower to flower, so does proud, haughty, arrogant Love flit from one beauty to another. He wounds one and heals another; in one he lights his torch, in another he awakens cruelty. As the bee, etc.

83 CORR. So you are determined . . . ?

ROB. In vain do you tempt me.

CORR. . . . to leave this palace . . . ?

ROB. I have been here too long, to my unhappiness.

CORR. . . . to abandon Costanza?

ROB. It is torture to have one's lost sweetheart near one.

CORR. And will you have the heart to do this?

ROB. I will force myself to.

CORR. But what will the fair lady say?

ROB. Let her lament her ill fortune.

CORR. She will spoil the rubies of her lips with sighing.

ROB. You can console her.

CORR. She will bedew the flowers of her cheeks with weeping.

ROB. I too shall weep with her.

CORR. And two hearts will be killed by a single farewell.

ROB. Corrado, you are cruel.

CORR. I should like you to be more faithful to your belovèd idol.

ROB. The fault is not in me, but in my stars.

CORR. Stand up to your fate with a strong spirit and an unruffled brow.

ROB. I seek a remedy for my woes, and not advice.

CORR. At least wait until . . .

ROB. . . . another lover takes from me the woman I adore, before my very eyes, and lights the abhorred candles before the sacred altars, and gives her his embrace in my stead!

CORR. Yes, just this, and then go where you will.

ROB. Cruel sacrifice, I do not want to behold thee. (*As* ROBERTO *starts to leave,* COSTANZA *arrives.*)

84 CORR. (*To* ROBERTO) Take, if you wish, your last farewell from these fair belovèd eyes, and then go away, if you can, wherever you will. Come back and admire these loving eyes, and then extinguish, if you can, the torch in your heart. Take, etc.

Scene ix
ROBERTO *and* COSTANZA

85 COST. Will you depart, o Roberto, from this palace, where you are leaving your heart with me and taking my heart with you? Will you steal thus my only remaining happiness, the sight of you? And perhaps were you going away without even speaking to me? without giving me a glance? without saying farewell to me? You are indeed cruel to your own heart and ungrateful to mine.

ROB. I should like to spare you such a tragic farewell; but, o Heavens, I cannot. I am forced to temper my cruel torment with your sufferings, and to mingle your sighs with mine.

COST. (Honor, tyrannical gods, what are you forcing me to do? Love, sweet tie, where are you taking me? Be less guilty, affections of my heart, if you are faithless.) Go, Roberto, and, since you are already leaving me guilty, know all my sin: this hand will belong to another, this heart to you.

ROB. Ah, say no more that you love me, if you wish me to betake myself far from you; your faithfulness is a great inducement to delay.

COST. I shall say it no more, my life. Go, yes, go. I too will hasten your departure; delay is a great temptation to my honor.

ROB. Costanza . . .

COST. Are you abandoning me?

ROB. This is what my fate and your destiny command.

COST. O Heaven!

ROB. Remember me; think . . .

COST. Roberto, no more, for you are killing me.

ROB. And you are now separating my soul from my soul.

86 Beautiful hand, I did not think . . .

COST. Fair right hand, I believed . . .

ROB. I would die
COST. I would have joy } in clasping thee,

BOTH. And yet I feel . . .

ROB. . . . every death . . .

COST. . . . every torment . . .

BOTH. . . . clasping your hand thus.

ROB. I shall go . . .

COST. I shall stay . . .

ROB. . . . but leaving you my heart . . .

COST. . . . but preserving my love for you . . .

BOTH. . . . in spite of that fate, which pitilessly has stolen . . .

ROB. . . . your faith from me.

COST. . . . my faith from you.
Beautiful, etc.

Scene x

GRISELDA, CORRADO *and the aforementioned.*

87 GRIS. (*To* COSTANZA) With such modest affection are you a consort to your bridegroom? (*To* ROBERTO) With such honorable respect do you come as a friend to the palace? Is this, is this the faith of marriage, the law of hospitality? On the day of his wedding, in his very dwelling, do you not love a husband? Do you not fear a king? O illicit love! o ultimate expression of contempt!

COST. (Wretch!)

ROB. (What advice!)

GRIS. Are you still silent? Do you still not answer?

Scene xi

GUALTIERO *and the aforementioned.*

88 GUAL. Griselda?

COST. (Woe is me!)

ROB. (I am done for!)

GUAL. Why are you angry? And you, fair souls, why are you confused?

GRIS. Must I say?

GUAL. (*To* GRISELDA) Tell me, what have you heard? What have you seen?

GRIS. Nothing, except for my destiny, always cruel, always pitiless towards me.

GUAL. Let Prince Corrado tell me what has happened; you are offensive to me, whether you speak or are silent.

CORR. You can hear in a few words, Sire.

ROB. (There is no escape!)

COST. (Alas, my fate!)

CORR. A reciprocal love unites the heart of Roberto and Costanza. Griselda heard their conversation, and saw their right hands clasped.

GUAL. Then why so much disdain? It is easy to see that you were born in the wilderness, Griselda. Am I perhaps expecting you to play the rôle of a scout, or of a maid and servant? Control your pride and keep to your duties.

GRIS. That zeal . . .

GUAL. I do not ask you for it.

GRIS. The respect . . .

GUAL. You owe it to my royal bride.

GRIS. Your honor, your glory . . .

GUAL. What does it matter to you if fair Costanza has more than one lover? that she divides her heart? that she loves either Roberto or Gualtiero as she wishes?

ROB. AND COST. (Ye gods, what do I hear?)

GUAL. Remember her rank . . .

GRIS. It is that of a queen.

GUAL. Your duty . . .

GRIS. It is that of a handmaiden.

GUAL. . . . and if sometimes you see her burn for another . . .

GRIS. My eyes will be blind.

GUAL. . . . if you hear her sigh . . .

GRIS. My ears will be deaf.

GUAL. . . . and if she lovingly takes Roberto's hand, do not get angry; but remember that Roberto and Costanza have loved each other since childhood, and have clasped each other's hands; and, as then, their love is still innocent.

GRIS. I shall carry out your lofty commands as I should, suffering and remaining silent. (Barbarous destiny of mine, I do not understand you!)

CORR. I, my lord, assure you that both your bride's and my brother's desire is innocent; that their hearts are modest; nor does their love offend your glory. (*Exit.*)

COST. (I tremble.)

ROB. (I am afraid.)

GUAL. Now let not your chaste love be extinguished by cold, meddlesome fear. I forgive certain affections, which are begotten by time and the heart, on the ground of character and age.

COST. I should not wish for forgiveness, if I had offended your honor and mine with a shadow of thought or intent.

ROB. A voluntary exile, such as I was taking . . .

GUAL. Be silent, for excuses displease me more than your love. By fleeing from Costanza, you are incurring guilt, Roberto; and you are more guilty, if you separate from him. Continue loving each other, and be faithful.

GUAL. Love was never a fault; it became a fault when it offended honesty. 89

COST. The ardor which I have in my heart . . .

ROB. The flame which is setting me on fire . . .

BOTH. . . . will always be chaste.

GUAL. (But yet my torment . . .

ROB. AND COST. (But yet my fright . . .

GRIS. (But yet my crime . . .

ALL FOUR. . . . is that same faithfulness.)

GUAL. (As long as an innocent affection burns in your bosoms . . .

GRIS. (As long as in the loving bosom, the heart is steadfast . . .

ROB. AND COST. . . . perhaps on my sighs . . .

GRIS. . . . perhaps on my torments . . .

GUAL. . . . perhaps on your troubles . . .

ALL FOUR. . . . Heaven will have pity.)

Love was never, etc.

Scene xii
COSTANZA.

90 COST. O gods, might what a gentle, flattering affection whispers to me in my heart be true? I no longer feel that inner torment which I felt before. I think of Gualtiero . . . I think of Corrado . . . enough. I do not understand myself; but in such sweet form, my hope cannot be deceiving me.

91 If I am fair, if I am beautiful, if I am faithful, my belovèd idol; I am fair, I am beautiful, I am faithful for you. Could I cease loving you? Could I think of abandoning you? I feel myself grow faint; I feel myself dying; it is not possible. If I am fair, etc.

Scene xiii
Amphitheater, being prepared for the wedding, with illuminations and other displays. GRISELDA.

92 GRIS. Finish, o servants, the grand solemn festival. Bring the day back to life with your lights; and let the palace, at its most cheerful, hear the wedding vows of its lord. It is the command of my Gualtiero that I myself should hasten and make more proud the bitter scene of my tragedies.

Last Scene
GUALTIERO, ROBERTO, OTTONE, COSTANZA, GRISELDA, *and* CORRADO *with* EVERARDO. *Knights, damsels, guards, and people as spectators.*

93 GUAL. Griselda?

GRIS. The only thing lacking is your sovereign command.

GUAL. I suffer endless torments every minute which keeps me from Costanza.

GRIS. You also once loved Griselda.

GUAL. Your baseness extinguished my bright flames.

GRIS. May they burn eternally for your noble bride. Ah, do not demand from her the rare example of my patience; it will be hard for Costanza, noble by blood, and not so accustomed to misfortune as I, a woman of base birth.

COST. (Oh, what goodness!)

ROB. (Oh, what virtue!)

GUAL. (My heart is breaking!)

CORR. (*Aside to* GUALTIERO) What more can you ask?

GUAL. The final proof of her firmness. Ottone?

OTT. Noble ruler . . .

GUAL. Come forward. And you, Griselda . . .

GRIS. Behold me ready to obey you.

CORR. (*To* GUALTIERO, *as above*) Ah, you see that you are not mistaken.

GRIS. Your fear is groundless.

CORR. She is, after all, only a woman.

GUAL. But such, that she might shame the stronger sex. (*To* GRISELDA) You have suffered a great deal; your courage is worthy of a reward; I have pity on you. You shall no longer be a shepherdess in the woods, Griselda, or a maid-servant at the court; but you shall be the bride of the faithful Ottone.

OTT. (Joy, do not kill me!)

GRIS. I, Ottone's . . . ?

GUAL. He is the foremost upholder of my scepter; he is the brightest ornament of Sicily; and such that he can share your nuptial couch after Gualtiero.

GRIS. I, Ottone's . . . ?

GUAL. Plight him your troth as his bride. Here is your Everardo, as well. I commanded him to be killed; but since a friendly fate decided to save him, let Ottone care for him, caress him, and love him.

GRIS. Ah, Sire . . .

GUAL. Obey; your king commands you.

GRIS. My King, my deity, once my husband and still my delight, you know whether I always made your orders my law. You yourself tell it; people, you tell it, you who beheld it. You deprived me of the kingdom, you sent me into forced exile, you expelled me from your couch and your throne. I returned, as a shepherdess, to the forest, and I came as a maid-servant to the palace. As a servant, I have hastened your nuptials. I have suffered sorrow, risk, shame, contempt, in short everything, without calling you pitiless, without accusing you as a ingrate. But will you marry me to Ottone? Shall my heart belong to another? my faith? my love? Ah, Gualtiero, forgive me; this, this, is the dear possession, which alone I have kept, free from your commands; I have lived as yours, and I shall die as yours, belovèd husband.

GUAL. (Tears, do not gush forth!) Why are you delaying any longer? Choose; Ottone, or death.

GRIS. Death, death, my lord. Servants, guards, seek my death in tortures, sharpen it in your swords, make it bitter in poisons. Who among you wishes the glory of the first blow? Ah, husband, I ask it from your hand (*kneels*) and I beg it at your feet. Send me to the Elysian fields as a shade proud of such a belovèd death, showing there my beautiful wounds, the effect first of your eyes, then of your arm.

GUAL. (No more, my heart, no more!) My wife, I embrace you!

OTT. (O wretched Ottone!)

PEOPLE. Hurrah for Griselda! Hurrah!

GUAL. People, who are guilty towards Heaven and towards your king, now you see what kind of a woman I chose as queen for you, as wife for myself. Her virtue, not her blood, makes her worthy of your plaudits and of my love. Now, with such repentance, I easily forgive your error.

OTT. Great King, the wrongdoing of the people is my fault alone. It was I who, impelled by love for Griselda, excited the kingdom several times to rebellion. My gifts were very influential among the vulgar herd, my example among the grandees; now I ask your pardon for a crime both serious and cruel.

GUAL. Your sorrow is enough for me, and I grant it to you.

CORR. Great-hearted pity!

COST. (*To* ROBERTO) What will happen to us?

ROB. I have hope, my belovèd.

GUAL. But you are silent, Griselda; and is your brow hardly glad at our happy destiny? Perhaps you do not believe in it? or perhaps is your joy not yet complete?

GRIS. To tell you the truth, I am unhappy over Costanza's fate; she is losing a king and a realm.

GUAL. Could a daughter be her father's bride?

GRIS. AND COST. What?

GUAL. Let Corrado tell the story.

CORR. (*To* GRISELDA) Yes, Costanza is your daughter for whose death you wept.

GRIS. (*Embracing* COSTANZA) O my daughter!

COST. O mother!

GRIS. My heart told me before now, and I did not understand it.

GUAL. You, my belovèd Roberto, do not steal from me all the love of Costanza, whom I now give you as your bride.

ROB. Your gift, o great King, makes me happy.

GUAL. (*To* GRISELDA) Come back with me now, my belovèd, on my royal throne.

CORR. AND OTT. And may Everardo be your heir, but a long time hence.

GUAL., GRIS., ROB., AND COST. Be crowned with flowers, chaste loves, and ask a torch some star from faith and beauty. Then, proclaiming our ardors to a thousand loving souls, sing, o chaste Loves, of constancy and beauty.

ALL. Be crowned, etc.

94

END OF THE DRAMA

290